Trying to Catch the Wind

Trying to Catch the Wind

Memoir of a Love That Was More Than Love

Josef N. Ferri

iUniverse, Inc.
Bloomington

TRYING TO CATCH THE WIND
MEMOIR OF A LOVE THAT WAS MORE THAN LOVE

iUniverse books may be ordered through booksellers or by contacting:

iUniverse
1663 Liberty Drive
Bloomington, IN 47403
www.iuniverse.com
1-800-Authors (1-800-288-4677)

Because of the dynamic nature of the Internet, any web addresses or links contained in this book may have changed since publication and may no longer be valid. The views expressed in this work are solely those of the author and do not necessarily reflect the views of the publisher, and the publisher hereby disclaims any responsibility for them.

Any people depicted in stock imagery provided by Thinkstock are models, and such images are being used for illustrative purposes only.

Certain stock imagery © Thinkstock.

ISBN: 978-1-4759-6913-9 (sc)
ISBN: 978-1-4759-6914-6 (hc)
ISBN: 978-1-4759-6915-3 (e)

Library of Congress Control Number: 2012924181

Printed in the United States of America

iUniverse rev. date: 3/28/2013

Table of Contents

Introduction ix

CHAPTER ONE

Summit of Mount Everest 1
Rupture 2
Kappa Phi 3
The Interview 6
Hearing a Discernible Voice Within 10
Traveling an Uncharted Road 12
The Working World/Breaking Away 13
The Windfall 16

CHAPTER TWO

Two Worlds Meet 19
Beer-Blast at the Lake 22
A Factory Worker's Shangri-la 23
Ride Back to Reality 24

CHAPTER THREE

Chance Encounter 28
The Highest High 30
Into the Path of a Predator/The Lowest Low 39
Fury in a Crowded Corridor 41
Teetotaler's Hangover 43
Visiting an Angel from a Dream 46

CHAPTER FOUR

Changing Direction/Walking the Well-Trodden Path 49
Growing Awareness/Blossoming Relationship 51
The Awakening and a Sacred Vow 54

CHAPTER FIVE

Renewed Acquaintances and a Nautical Misadventure	58
Her Voice: Sustenance for My Soul	63
Pilgrimage to a Forbidden Place	66
A Vision in Daylight	68

CHAPTER SIX

A Wall Is Taken Down/A Foreign World Is Revealed	71
Focused Goals and a Renewed Purpose	73
Humble Symbol of Eternal Love	77

CHAPTER SEVEN

Meeting the Last Familial Piece of the Puzzle	80
A First Step toward Independence	82
A Last Parental Interference/Our Great Escape	86

CHAPTER EIGHT

A Brave New World/Creating Paradise	88
Building Bridges and Seeking Answers	90
The Gift: A Sacrifice for My Beloved	97
Desperately Searching for Permanent Solutions	99
A Hint of Spring and Rebirth Again	100

CHAPTER NINE

An Olive Branch from a Past World	103
Summer of Sun, Sand, and Fun/Autumn of Changes, Challenges, and New Problems	105
Self-Discovery, Death, and a Renewed Rift	108

CHAPTER TEN

A Miscalculation, Consequences, and Confusion	112
Foregone Conclusions Jeopardized	115
A Family Conflict Laid to Rest/Petty Jealousies Arise	116

CHAPTER ELEVEN

A New Spring Approaches	121
Into the Vibrant Social Scene	123
Political Pressure Grows/A Generation Seeks Escape	126
A Magical Door Opens/A Roof Caves In	131

CHAPTER TWELVE

Nightlife and Laughter as an Oasis	135
Sharing a Special Place of Inspiration	139
Locating an Outlaw Commando	141
Foreign Experience: A Seed Is Planted	142

CHAPTER THIRTEEN

To the Edge of Death Valley	147
Epiphany in Purgatory	149
Afflicted Exile	151

CHAPTER FOURTEEN

The Shadow Cast across a Lifetime	154
Living an Examined Life	155
An Unanticipated Miracle	158
Searching for Her Double	159

CHAPTER FIFTEEN

Two Worlds Converge Again	163
Paradise Revisited	164
The Journey with a Moral Compass and No Map	166
The Impenetrable Fog Is Lifted	170
A Personal Dichotomy and a Mistaken Choice	172

CHAPTER SIXTEEN

Dwelling in the Valley and the Infinite Void	177

INTRODUCTION

Matters of the heart are quite subjective and touch people very differently. Some people move from one lover to another almost seamlessly, with little aftereffect from the previous relationship. Yet for others on the opposite end of the emotional spectrum, the loss of their beloved is devastating, almost crippling. Their lives sometimes teeter on the edge of existence. When it comes to discussions of such things, everyone has an opinion. The following story is but one. First, allow me to mention several points.

First love is one of the great positive human experiences. It energizes all our senses and infuses optimism about life to the highest level imaginable. For most of us, this great gift occurs in our youth, about the time we are in transition into physical adulthood. This experience comes too soon to be fully appreciated or understood—and, more significantly, before we have enough life experiences and maturity to make the relationship work.

In most cases, first love is a transitory relationship, a kind of romantic boot camp that helps us prepare for later amorous experiences. It always hurts terribly to lose a first love, and there seems to be a lasting residual effect, one filled with pain and regrets. There is also an almost universal sense that a first relationship was ended prematurely by uncontrollable and unanticipated forces. Reluctantly, most people heal and move on in search of another love. What we learn from those encounters often helps us with subsequent lovers.

Finding someone who shares similar beliefs, passions, and views of life and the world is at the core of the relationships most people seek. Such a relationship is commonly referred to as one between *soul mates*. A soul mate is a reflection of yourself, a person who embodies and resonates an aura that instantly is in sync with what you feel inside and that affirms your very being. Soul mates are a perfect complement to your existence, and their presence in your world completes the incomplete circle of life you're looking to find. With such a person, you feel a wholeness that is necessary for lasting happiness. You can't conceive of a life without that special someone. In the case of *real* soul mates, both people must share the same awareness, the same elation, and the same joy in the presence of the other. If there is not an almost instant, mutual recognition of this seemingly perfect symmetry by both people, they are not true soul mates.

When these two elements of *first love* and *soul mate* converge, the relationship is magnified many times, and its importance is substantially heightened. Depending on the individual circumstances of the two lovers, this dual impact of the first lover/soul mate is powerfully enhanced and its effect much longer lasting. If the relationship doesn't work out, if the relationship is ended by nefarious inscrutable and unforeseen forces, the resulting consequence may cast a lifelong shadow over one's existence.

By definition, there can only be one first love. However, it's possible to have more than one soul mate. This latter possibility, of losing one soul mate and then finding another, is a key motivation for most people to move on with their lives. The pain and sense of loss eventually fade to a point where their hearts are once again receptive to the possibility of another love. But replacing a first love that is also a soul mate is a far more complex situation, one that sometimes isn't ever overcome.

To see a powerful example of the effect of the loss of a soul mate (and a likely first love as well), one need only read Edgar Allen Poe's great poem "Annabel Lee" (see pp. xiii – xiv). As a young man of only thirteen, I read that poem in grade school and was immediately and profoundly touched. Although I had only gone through a number of *puppy loves* (finite infatuations) in my young life, I somehow recognized the difference and enormous impact of the type of love Poe described in his magnum opus. I wanted to feel and experience the power and force of such a love. His great poem became the secret standard and benchmark by which I would gauge my future romantic relationships. What did it feel like to have that sort of a deep and all-encompassing love? And would the bar I set for myself be too high, too unattainable to be fulfilled?

Several years later, when I began to cross the magical and mysterious threshold into physical manhood, I was enthralled by the first commercial release of a song by a young poet-singer which I felt captured an intense sentiment similar to Poe's great poem. Donovan's song "Catch The Wind" struck my heart with the same sort of power and impact. It energized and spurred my desire to find such a fantastic love. The following true-life story is about my search for, discovery of, and loss of my first love and soul mate.

The details and great lasting pain of my lost love have been buried deep within my heart and mind, beneath decades of learning, searching, and experiencing as much life as I could. Along my journey, I've met many amazing people (some famous, some remarkable), visited and spent time in some breathtaking locations around the world, loved other women, and never stopped feeling and pursuing the ever-moving, ever-changing, and ever-wondrous *life force* that George Bernard Shaw described.

The life force is an intellectual and emotional energy that is both understandable and mysterious, both of the moment yet timeless. It is of the past, present, and future, and it is both static and moving at the same time. It's an awareness of *self* being touched by something that transcends time, an esoteric continuum that is endless and infinite. Once you've been touched by it, you feel an inner glow created by the awareness that some profound truth has penetrated your very soul.

This tremendous type of experience can be prompted by an innocent baby's smile, a magnificent sunset, a great novel, a masterpiece in an art gallery, an exquisite poem, a moving performance of a profound play, the sound created by a remarkable musician—or the feeling of love shared with your soul mate. If you feel an incredible surge of life and joy and an almost overwhelming happiness by any of these sort of things, then you are enveloped in the life force.

Intellectually, you are aware that you are feeling something beyond the confines of time and that you, at that instant, are a finite vessel through which the life force passes as it moves toward a distant future. Being in contact with this force gives you an enormous sense of empowerment and a special joy. And you realize that you can actively pursue this force—if you choose. The pursuit of truth and beauty at the heart of the wondrous life force has been the singular pure joy of my life, the grand counterbalance to the enormous loss of my greatest love.

But now in my later life, as I assess and evaluate my existence, my one greatest disappointment has found its way to the top of my thoughts and onto paper. It is a story—my personal story—and I wanted it to be told and shared. My belief and hope is that my story will touch other people with a similar experience, to let them know that even though they've lost someone special and important, there is still a reason to live on, to continue to seek beauty and meaning in their lives. And, most importantly, I hope my story will show that love for a lost soul mate *can* live on within a special place in the heart. The love of soul mates is an emotional and spiritual bond and will conjoin them together forever, regardless of their physical separation or their love for others. Our capacity for *love* can truly be boundless and timeless, and it is one of the great pathways to feeling some of the joy of the mystic and endless life force.*

As for me, I will never stop loving that young woman in my life.

---

* Some of the names of people in this story have been changed. A special thanks to Donovan Leitch who personally gave me permission to use the lyrics of his songs which appear in the story.

Annabel Lee

It was many and many a year ago,
In a kingdom by the sea,
That a maiden there lived ... whom you may know
By the name of Annabel Lee;
And this maiden she lived with no other thought
Than to love and be loved by me.

She *was a child and* I *was a child,*
In this kingdom by the sea,
But we loved with a love that was more than love—
I and my Annabel Lee—
With a love that the wingéd seraphs of Heaven
Coveted her and me.

And this was the reason that, long ago,
In this kingdom by the sea,
A wind blew out of a cloud by night
Chilling my Annabel Lee;
So that her highborn kinsmen came
And bore her away from me,
To shut her up in a sepulchre
In this kingdom by the sea.

The angels, not half so happy in Heaven,
Went envying her and me:
Yes! That was the reason (as all men know,
In this kingdom by the sea)
That the wind came out of a cloud, chilling
And killing my Annabel Lee.

But our love it was stronger by far than the love
Of those who were older than we—
Of many far wiser than we—
And neither the angels in Heaven above
Nor the demons down under the sea,
Can ever dissever my soul from the soul
Of the beautiful Annabel Lee;

For the moon never beams without bringing me dreams
Of the beautiful Annabel Lee;
And the stars never rise but I see the bright eyes
Of the beautiful Annabel Lee;
And so, all the night-tide, I lie down by the side
Of my darling, my darling, my life and my bride,
In her sepulchre there by the sea—
In her tomb by the side of the sea.

—Edgar Allen Poe

Chapter One

⌐

Summit of Mount Everest

It was a perfect late spring night: warm with the scent of flowers and freshly cut grass emanating from all directions in the almost mystical darkness. The road we were on was smooth, winding, and surprisingly free of traffic, a far cry from the volume it would experience in exactly one short month, when the Independence Day exodus from the bustling Rust Belt city thirty miles away would begin in earnest. When we slowed or stopped at the few stop signs and turns along our impromptu route, we could feel slight radiant heat rising off the muffler and modest engine of my small white Yamaha motorcycle, which transformed the burning gasoline, mixed with motor oil, into a fine Japanese perfume.

Our senses were heightened to glorious, unimaginable levels. The joy of the last four hours had exceeded the greatest expectations of any of our youthful dreams. As if by a fantastic miracle, we found ourselves in the midst of our most cherished, secret dream and could feel the hands of omnipotent destiny gently embracing our young souls. The lifelong path to this moment, too often filled with disappointments, made the present moment that much more sublime. We both felt the certainty of knowing we had found our soul mate, and the sense of that acknowledgment sent our youthful spirits into indescribable ecstasy that would last a lifetime. A great love story was beginning, not in the pages of a book but in our very lives. We felt it; we knew it. This was to be the first chapter of a story that would touch many lives, affect many people, and resonate for at least two lifetimes.

While I drove through the serene night on that peaceful road, I could feel her arms wrapped tightly around my waist and her perfect body pressing against my back with her helmetless head resting gently near my right shoulder. The image of her molded against me danced in my head as the somewhat cooling night air glanced off my face, chest, and legs. Her body heat warming my back was tangible evidence, empirical proof, that the last four hours were not a mirage or some wild, fanciful dream but rather the beginning of a holy pilgrimage, an odyssey to a place that lovers dream of, relentlessly search for, and only seldom enter.

Although we were young in years, the journey to that fateful night seemed to have taken an eternity. The separate paths we traveled to reach our first night together were as different as our backgrounds. We had radically different family situations. It was no less a miracle that two such fearless romantics would be paired together in perfect harmony, on an absolutely flawless night, in remarkably enlightened conversation away from our respective peer influences and restrictive family lives.

Rupture

In August 1964, less than a year before, my mother, who was at the end of her emotional rope, exiled my father for the final time. What choice did she have? After finding out that his absences on drinking sprees had the hidden agenda of seeing another woman, who had given birth to an illegitimate daughter and was pregnant with a son, Mom digested the horrible reality and began the next chapter of her life and ours. My oldest sister, Pat, was already married and gone from our home. But my other sisters, Linda and Camille, my brother, Al, and I were all still in school and living with our mother.

The trauma of those events, which took place over four years, had scarred all of us. Each of us five children reacted differently to the catastrophic memories. Every one of us was profoundly affected, and, as I look back across the landscapes of each of our lives, I see that all of us suffered the consequences of that failed relationship to various degrees. The loss of a significant father figure hurt me deeply, leaving a void that could never quite be filled by a surrogate.

I was intelligent and analytical and came to understand that, in a twisted sort of way, my father had given me the ultimate reverse role model of what to be as a husband and a father. I would know, firsthand, the cause and effect of a broken family. In those painful days, observing my father's aberrant behavior and its dire consequences, I learned introspection and self-examination. That sad time ignited my intense examination of all aspects of my life. I started questioning everything. I needed to know *why* things were as they were.

As a student, I had demonstrated an inquisitive mind and had achieved good grades. My search for truth and knowledge was accelerated by the troubles at home. I saw pain in my brother, sisters, and mother and needed to find answers to the questions that kept surfacing in my head. The search for answers began in earnest at that time and would cast its impact upon my entire life. With my heightened sensitivity, it was only natural for me to develop a growing interest in art, literature, music, and especially poetry, which rapidly captured my eager, thirsty imagination. On the one hand, I had a failing family life with all its calamitous consequences. But on the other hand, I developed a growing, insatiable hunger for learning and living life, and I began an unending quest to know myself and my place in the complex world.

By the time I graduated from high school, we had lived in nine apartments and I had attended eight different schools scattered across three sides of the city. Although I was uprooted often, I managed to make new friends and adapt to every new environment. I was athletic and did well in class. When I was a sophomore in high school, as my manhood began to emerge, my social life came alive. Friday night dances, parties with other teenagers, hanging out at pool halls, and visiting restaurants all began to be a part of our social scene.

Kappa Phi

In the 1960s, a phenomenon began in Western New York that lasted for seven or eight years. High school students started forming Greek fraternities for guys and sororities for the young ladies. Most of these fraternities and sororities were limited to particular schools, but some became the envy of all the others. Fraternities were not gangs for fighting but rather exclusive clubs for partying.

Without question, the most popular and successful fraternity in the entire era of these organizations in all of Western New York was Kappa

Phi. Every fraternity and sorority aspired to be like KΦ. Its members were a wide assortment of athletes, musicians, bright kids, funny kids, cool kids, and well-known kids. Through the process of careful selection of individuals and mergers with other popular and cool frats, Kappa Phi emerged as the ultimate in-crowd. The best sororities sought to have joint (excuse the double entendre) meetings with KΦ, and no other frat dared to disparage or physically challenge Kappa Phi members. It was an axiom of the era: every frat tried to be as cool and successful as Kappa Phi, every guy wanted to be a member of it, and every young lady wanted to date a member. It was the benchmark against which all other frats and sororities were measured.

Once a frat was organized and had enough members who paid weekly dues, quite often an unfurnished apartment was rented. Members donated chairs, rugs, lamps, old couches, and anything they could find or scavenge to furnish their frat-house apartments. Parties were held where drinking was sanctioned and sexual encounters were encouraged. It was a prelude for the upcoming free-love movement, but with a membership restriction.

My best friend in 1963–1964 was Artie P., who attended Hutch-Tech High School and was friends with an influential member of KΦ. Joe L., who was variously known as Joe Hawk, the Hawk, or simply Hawk, had invited Artie to pledge for Kappa Phi. Artie, who was closer to me than my own brother, wanted me to be a pledge along with him, so he asked Hawk if I could pledge too. Hawk replied that I could pledge with Artie only after he met me in person to see if I had the right stuff.

Artie excitedly gave me the news and told me I was to meet the Hawk at the weekly dance at Mount Major Hall on Friday night. Artie was certain that I would be impressive enough to be asked to join the exclusive ranks of Kappa Phi. I didn't give it a second thought and looked forward to meeting this legendary person, whom Artie idealized. Throughout the time I worked at Scadutto's Corner Market with Artie, he raved about Hawk's prowess as a street fighter and his *couthness* (Artie's word) with women. He worshipped Joe Hawk, and to be a part of KΦ was Artie's greatest dream.

On Fridays, Artie and I worked at Scadutto's after school for a few hours before going home to get ready for Mount Major. It invariably was the highlight of the week and was talked about daily at school. Once in a while there was a fight, but usually it was a place just to have fun, hear live music, socialize, and dance.

On the designated Friday, Artie and I arrived wearing bleeding madras shirts, tight white jeans with short pants legs, Addler socks, and British Walker shoes and heavily doused with English Leather or Canoe cologne. No two madras shirts were alike, and Addlers came in every conceivable color. All of us looked similar but different, and all of us attempted to be unique within the range of the popular style. Once we passed through the doorway and paid our one-dollar admission, we carved our way through the center of the gyrating crowd. The stage was on our right, and West Ferry Street was directly behind us as we angled past the pulsating dancers.

Artie locked his sights on someone in front of us and moved quickly toward him with me following close behind. Suddenly, Artie came to an abrupt stop and pushed his hand out toward a well-groomed, dark-haired, deep-staring young man. Artie said his name in a proud and reverent manner: "Hawk!" immediately followed by: "I want you to meet my friend, Ferris" (Artie's nickname for me). As Hawk shook my hand, he looked at me intensely and said: "Artie's told me a lot about you. How do you do?"

Hawk's voice was raspy like that of someone who had just been to a concert and had been yelling too much. I told him I was glad to finally meet him too, and inquired about his raspy voice by asking, "Do you have a sore throat?"

As he said, "No," I detected a slight look of embarrassment on his part. We spoke about general things for several awkward minutes and then walked off in different directions. The interview was over.

I was furious with Artie. When we were away from Joe Hawk, I told Artie I couldn't believe he hadn't told me about Hawk's voice. Artie, in his blind idolatry of Hawk, had completely forgotten that one little, pertinent detail. I was fairly certain I was not going to be invited to pledge for KΦ after my embarrassing but innocent *faux pas*. It would've been great to be in that frat, but my world wouldn't end if I wasn't. Besides, I had been asked to join several other frats; although none was near the stature of Kappa Phi, they would suffice if need be, or so I thought. It was going to be a large helping of sour grapes.

The Interview

After school on Monday, Artie came by my house to tell me about the aftermath of the Friday meeting with Hawk. I expected the worst but was surprised to hear that Hawk wanted both of us to come to the next weekly frat meeting to be interviewed by the whole membership before being formally accepted as pledges.

The night of our interview was the next night, Tuesday, at seven in the carriage house of the president of Kappa Phi, Rick S. He was the ultra-cool leader of the iconic local band the Buffalo Beatles. Artie and I walked to the meeting dressed in our best Friday night Mount Major outfits. Both of us were excited about this upcoming mysterious and frightening ritual. We had a date with fate, and if it went well our remaining high school time, two and a half years, would be filled with incredible adventures and memories.

My understanding of the process, according to Artie, was that each pledge candidate would be called by name to stand in the center of the seated assemblage of thirty or so members. Each aspirant would be questioned and tested for poise and grace under verbal fire. What questions would be asked was unknown, but nothing was out of bounds. The half dozen candidates selected for this night's festivities were unaware of what they'd be asked and the order of who was to be interviewed. And not everyone would be selected to pledge. We had no foreknowledge of any particulars of the criteria. It was all quite secretive and intimidating.

Rick's carriage house was an old nineteenth-century wooden structure located behind his family house on Rhode Island Street. It had electrical service but no heating system. Human body heat warmed the room on this mid-November night. The members sat on odds and ends including chairs, wooden grates, and old benches. A discernible patina of dust coated every object and surface, save the people in the building. Rick sat behind a beat-up old desk with Angelo M., his loyal VP, by his side. One by one, the pledge prospects were introduced and fielded the questions randomly hurled at them by the feisty fraternity brothers in the gallery. It was quickly apparent this was not a *normal* interview that sought serious responses. It was a comedy show, and the pledges-to-be became the straight men for off-the-cuff, freewheeling dialogue.

Some of the wannabe pledges were turned into verbal punching bags and were so unsettled that they wouldn't be asked to pledge. Once the interlocutors perceived vulnerability in a potential candidate, they would pounce on it and rapidly pursue a line of questioning to test the mettle of that prospective pledge.

"So, your girlfriend is so-and-so?" asked one frat brother.

"Yes, we've been going together for eight months," proudly proclaimed the candidate.

"Are you in a serious relationship?" someone else asked.

"Oh, yes, we're very serious!" said the unsuspecting interviewee with great pride.

Then, from yet another direction, a frat brother sharply and loudly inquired: "Have you slept together?"

Instantly, the pledge prospect's poise completely vanished, and he was faced with a hopeless choice. If he said yes, the world (and his girlfriend) would know he had revealed his most private experience. If he answered no, he would appear to be inexperienced and unworldly in front of this notoriously worldly group. He was dead on arrival. All his composure was gone, and the imaginary exit sign on the door of the carriage house flashed in bright red neon.

Artie's interview went smoothly because Hawk directed the rather tame questioning. Artie's wholehearted love of everything Kappa Phi was instantly apparent, and he was quickly returned to the viewer's gallery to watch my interrogation.

My name was called, and I stepped into the center of the seated gathering. "What school do you attend?" someone asked.

"Grover Cleveland," I responded.

"Do you play any sports?" another member queried.

"Football and track," I offered in an even tone of voice. The line of questioning was benign so far, and my responses were close-ended and nonprovocative. But I knew that if they got a whiff of blood, the tone and nature of the inquiries would get quite harsh.

Luckily, Phil L. then asked me: "Do you have a job?"

"Yes, I work with Artie P. at Scadutto's Market during the winter, and I have a summer job," I matter-of-factly stated.

Phil innocently rejoined: "What's your summer job?" I worked with a group of very clever, bright Jewish kids, most from educated families, who had a real sense of linguistic panache. So my response to Phil's wonderful setup question was to say what my Jewish friends would say when asked the same question. I knew the answer I was about to articulate would turn the tables on my fun-seeking interlocutors. "I'm a concessionaire at the Buffalo Zoological Society."

Immediately a din of questions erupted in the viewing gallery. Everyone began asking their neighbors what my response meant. You could hear ripples of the word "concessionaire" bandying about the room like a flock of startled pigeons. After a few moments, as the reverberating echo of the word "concessionaire" died out, Phil looked at me with an extremely puzzled look on his face. Once I saw his blank expression and perceived the whole assemblage anxiously awaiting a simple translation, I said in a loud, deadpan, slow voice: "I-sell-peanuts-at-the-zoo!"

The room exploded in reels of laughter, and I could hear many members repeating my words "peanuts-at-the-zoo." My little self-deprecating comment had accomplished my intended goal. None of the other frat members was going to get a louder laugh, so after a few more harmless questions, I was returned to the viewing gallery to watch the remaining potential pledges face their verbal Waterloo. Half of us were asked to pledge; the other three were sent off to join less significant frats or to pretend they never really wanted to pledge for Kappa Phi anyway.

I kept my powers of acute observation to myself and made no more innocent blunders by sharing my *gift*. Artie and I made it into the fraternity after six weeks of groveling and grueling pledging. We became certified fraternity brothers with the most dynamic group of young men of the era in Western New York. There was Rick S., who was president of KΦ and lead singer of the Buffalo Beatles, Kenny S. (a.k.a. the Goose), Bobby G. (a.k.a. the Greek), and other nonband members with equally colorful nicknames: Weasel, Buzz, Squirrel, Nippers, Mule, and, of course, Hawk. Almost all were charismatic, and many were multidimensional: athletic, academically bright, street cool, and popular with both guys and girls. The process of selection seemed deliberately strict and purposeful to perpetuate a certain chemistry and aura. All new members who were selected added various facets to the organization.

The one major, noteworthy episode of our pledge days was one of those sensational escapades that has all the earmarks and promise of greatness but ends up being *much ado about nothing*. As pledges, we were required to act like servants for all the members of Kappa Phi and to comply with all their reasonable requests: doing errands, performing servile tasks, and being nauseatingly polite (saying, "Yes, sir," "No, sir," etc.). While we were pledging, Kappa Phi rented an apartment on Connecticut Street, which was converted into our frat house. A Saturday night open house/beer blast party was scheduled.

Saturdays were always our busiest days at Scadutto's grocery store. So after our long workday had ended, Artie and I went to our respective homes, cleaned up, and rendezvoused outside my house, since it was closer to the frat house. Both of us were wildly excited about the open party and the incredible orders we had been given by Hawk. He told us each of us had to capture a pair of girl's panties at the party. The prospect of such a mission caused a wave of teenage titillation in both of us. Exactly how this mission would happen in reality was beyond our grasp, but the naked thought of trying raised our excitement substantially.

Because of our Saturday work schedule and the time needed to get ready, we found ourselves approaching Connecticut Street at just about nine p.m. Once we turned onto the street, we saw a sight neither of us had ever seen. There were people, perhaps several hundred strong, stretching for three city blocks from where we were all the way to our frat house. The confusing part was that the throng was not going toward the party but rather away from it.

We asked some of them what was going on, and the reply shattered our anticipating, enthusiastic hearts. We were told that the party had grown so big, so loud, and so wild that the police were called in and it was busted. Everyone was exiled. Nobody could ever remember a party of this sort reaching such monumental proportions. Poor Artie and I were left with a now-cancelled order that had levitated our expectations into the stratosphere. It was a goal that was unattainable, and we ended up like two social refugees from the promised land at the old Your Host Restaurant with other nonfrat friends, left imagining what might have been. We ended our night by ordering coffee and French fries with gravy as a way to divert our attention away from our mission, now impossible. It didn't work.

Hearing a Discernible Voice Within

Back in those days, in my family's bedlam, as my manhood and physical maturity began to manifest, I found myself moving toward the intellectual realm as much as the physical realm with its allure of sexual encounters with the opposite sex. The latter was a significant part of my being, but the former was equally influential. My friends wanted to have sexual liaisons with attractive women, and so did I. But I wanted to go beyond the physical sphere, to have meaningful conversations about life, music, books, and poetry. After the predictable crescendo of physical passion, which gives way to a special calm, I wanted to talk about ideas and the constant redefining mystery of life, to try to quench the unquenchable thirst for answers in our increasingly confusing world. Whereas my friends sought to make love, I sought to find love. The physical and intellectual realms coexisted side by side within me, not in opposition but rather as two compatible forces driving all my actions.

For most of my friends, physical climax was enough. Their lives seemed to revolve around that sole purpose. They worked jobs, they would marry, they would share sexual intimacy with their marriage partners, and they would have children and live together in their family-owned houses. But so many would drift into side relationships and infidelity that it would be rare to see anyone remain with one person for a lifetime. It was as if the lure of their physical desire superseded all other aspects of their being. The one-dimensional purpose of those relationships would decline, and inevitable consequences would follow.

Instinctively, I avoided relationships predicated solely on pure physical consequence and convenience. I longed to meet someone on the same physical and intellectual levels I was living through at this critical, impressionistic time. Of course, I had short-term relationships born of physical attraction. I, too, was driven by testosterone, but I had some sort of internal gyroscope that directed me away from entrapment and compromise. For me, it was exciting to discuss poetry, the civil rights movement (which was on the front pages of every newspaper), religion, the validity of the escalating Vietnam *conflict*, and the new music that was capturing the energetic skepticism of my generation as we witnessed the madness of the world enveloping all of America.

I had discovered my inner voice and the ability to engage my particular intellectual prowess. It was an internal island that gave me a unique province where a rich form of reward would be found, a place where I could find refuge from the increasingly confusing outer world where I physically dwelled. It was an impenetrable fortress of freedom and power, a source of endless fascination fueled by pure ideas and thought. It was a place where material things had little influence, and, I would discover later in life, it was a near-infinite reservoir of accessible memories of places, events, and people in my life. While the energy and power of my inner voice grew, I found myself with a heightened desire to connect with my female counterpart who searched for the same joy and amazement of intellectual revelation and self-awareness.

I was given no guiding path to follow in the life before me, but I felt the courage and optimism within to chart my own way. I was going to redefine my world, to take control of my life, and get to a special destination. I knew I would succeed, but I also knew I needed a soul mate to be with me. Without one, reaching my destination would be a hollow victory.

The painful upheaval of my home life reared its wretched face every day after the end of my parents' marriage. I swore to myself that I could never, and would never, hurt a woman as my father had done to my mother. The pain she felt and the sight of tears falling from her beautiful green eyes pierced my heart deeply. How could such an angel, who gave herself so completely to her husband and children, be punished so cruelly? I could not erase her tears, but I vowed to myself to never, ever be the cause of tears and pain like that when I met my soul mate. This inner oath to myself was another defining moment for me.

My eleventh year of school was a direct centrifugal spin-off of my parent's marital breakup. After the fall football season and a dismal, depressing Christmas in the poverty-stricken, dysfunctional home of our broken family, I became restless and yielded to the turmoil and confusion within. I quit high school in February 1965. Some force within me drove me to step off the merry-go-round of routine life. I needed to walk away from the assembly line of life to gather my thoughts and discover a clarity that could guide me.

My departure came as a shock to my teachers, who seemed stunned by the news. Bright kids who were obviously college bound didn't quit high school. One teacher who taught math and had a nasty Jesuit background tried to alter my path by informing me that "A high percentage of dropouts never finish school."

His words made no impression on me. He didn't know me and never would. Useless statistics did not apply to me. I dismissed his well-intentioned attempt as just another abstract mathematical equation that fell well short of the shores of the island I inhabited. Mathematics was his answer, not mine.

Traveling an Uncharted Road

But I'm just a soul whose intentions are good
Oh Lord, please don't let me be misunderstood
From: "Don't Let Me Be Misunderstood" by The Animals

In those days, if you quit high school and were under seventeen years old, you had to attend night school and have a full-time day job. Night school classes were attended by an assortment of older people there to get their diplomas, which would allow them to get better jobs and bragging rights as high school graduates. Other students, the younger ones, were there because of their lack of social skill, poor interpersonal behavior, or failure to apply an academic work ethic. I happened to be an oddball case: a good student clearly interested in learning whose focus had led to self-exile from the normal, regimented classrooms of my peers. A powerful darkness from within influenced my inner world, and I obeyed its directive.

Night school was interesting back then. Classes were smaller than regular day school. The fact that people were usually so tired from either working a job or hanging around all day meant that the elements of tension and conflict were all but gone. The teachers who taught classes were there to help the diverse group get through the course work while supplementing their modest income as teachers. The energy level of the teachers was also diminished by the long day. Everyone had a unique reason for being there, and all seemed to capitulate to the common goal.

The Working World/Breaking Away

My mandatory day job, my first full-time forty-hour-per-week job, was as a delivery boy delivering Photostat copies to advertising agencies and other specialty customers. In 1965, the copy machine did not exist in most businesses, and the idea of instant copies was not part of the business world. My employer, Pleger and Stevenson, would take artwork for advertising, hand-drawn architecture drawings and the like, place them on a large metal table, and then raise or lower a specially mounted overhead camera to take pictures of these items. The film from this camera was rapidly developed and printed. Copies were miraculously produced in mere hours. My job was to pick up and deliver the material on a bicycle through crowded, traffic-clogged downtown streets. I was paid the minimum wage of one dollar per hour (forty dollars per week). On especially cold, snowy days, I would walk to and from our customers' offices.

Today forty dollars per week sounds like a pittance, but back then when my friends had an allowance of three dollars per week, I was making a fortune. Thirty-four dollars after taxes allowed me to buy better clothes and go to dances through the front doors. But there was a stigma, at least in my mind, attached to the image of me riding a bicycle to earn those bountiful dollars.

Bicycles were strictly and narrowly associated with childhood and immaturity in those days. Cool people or grown-ups didn't ride bicycles. Children, immigrants, and impoverished, desperate people rode bicycles—and never in busy downtown Buffalo. Any association to the self-powered two-wheeler diminished one's self-image and thwarted the desire to be taken seriously on many other levels. It was one of those annoying paradoxes. On one hand, I made decent money, but I had to be on a bicycle to do it. The saving grace was that during the time I was pedaling through the hectic downtown streets, all the people I associated with were in classrooms, and I managed to never see or be seen by anyone I knew.

My job entailed riding to a particular business to pick up material and instructions for their copies and then returning to my Washington Street office. Pleger and Stevenson had their office on the sixth floor. When you entered their building, which was more of an industrial property, there was an open-ceiling freight elevator operated by a kindly

African American worker. Near the entrance to the elevator was a staircase that went all the way up to the top floor, where Pleger and Stevenson was located. There was a small problem on my first day of work.

Since preschool, I had an intense phobia of elevators, roller coasters, and heights in general. My mother occasionally took me on errands in downtown Buffalo when I was a preschooler and brought me to City Hall on one occasion. They had the fastest moving, quickest-stopping elevators I ever rode. The sensation was so harrowing that I was completely freaked out. Years and years passed, but I could not be coaxed into an elevator.

Now in 1965, just before my seventeenth birthday, I was hired by a company whose office was nestled in the sixth-floor clouds. I had three choices on my first day of work. I could return to the unemployment office and request to be hired by a business located on the first floor; I could attend a superfast psychoanalysis session to cure me; or, lastly, I could bypass the elevator for the staircase. The last choice was the simplest and fastest solution, which I enthusiastically embraced.

When I entered the Washington Street *skyscraper* on my first day of work, I said good morning to the elevator operator and walked past him to the staircase, which took me up to my new employer on the sixth floor. I was given a list of contacts and the key to the lock on my old, beat-up Huffy bicycle. Instead of pressing the button for the elevator, I picked up my two-wheel relic, hoisted it over my shoulder, and descended the stairs with no problem at all. When I passed the puzzled elevator operator as I left the building, I said good-bye.

The first phase of my new job was a snap, and I felt a false sense of confidence about my easy solution to that elevator thing. I soon discovered that many of my stops were located numerous floors above my sixth-floor office at Pleger and Stevenson. I stubbornly found the staircase at every location and marched up and down to their office. I walked up eight, ten, fourteen, eighteen flights of stairs at a time to pick up or drop off Photostat material. When I arrived at my Washington Street building, I would walk by our elevator operator and charge up the six flights of stairs to unload and reload. Whenever I passed the elevator operator, he looked at me with a combination of wonder and confusion. For two days, this pattern continued.

Finally, on the third day, the kindhearted elevator operator called me over. He asked me if I worked for Pleger and Stevenson on the sixth floor. I said yes. He asked me if my job required going to their customers scattered all over downtown on all different floors of the many office buildings. Again, I simply said yes.

"Do you take elevators in all those other buildings?" he said with genuine concern.

I looked at him as if guilty of some minor infraction and confessed, "No."

"*Good God!* You mean to tell me you've been climbing up and down scores of stairwells in all those buildings for two days?"

With a look of embarrassment, I again simply said, "Yes."

"Why, son, why?" he asked with a look of concerned shock. He knew I had probably climbed a few hundred flights of stairs in the past two days.

"The motion of elevators makes my stomach queasy," I confessed.

"Look," he said, "let me take you up in my open-ceiling freight elevator. I'll go real slowly, and you'll get used to it. It won't make you sick." As much as I enjoyed the physical exercise of climbing countless hundreds of flights of stairs, I decided I would give this generous offer a whirl. To my surprise, I felt no queasiness at all. This compassionate stranger had opened a new world for me. I immediately transferred my courage from the elevator on Washington Street to all elevators in the downtown Buffalo area. I was miraculously cured of my phobia of elevators forever.

And once I was no longer afraid of riding elevators, my fear of heights vanished as well. Shortly after my breakthrough, I found myself on one of the upper floors of the old Marine Midland building. I had to meet an architect at his desk by windows facing southward. I picked up his work to be brought back to Pleger and Stevenson and casually gazed in wonder past him out his windows. I was transfixed by the extraordinary view. It was as if I was an eagle soaring in the heavens and could see for miles and miles in all directions. I had never been up in any of the tall buildings in downtown Buffalo and had never seen such an amazing view live. Over four decades later, I can still recall my feeling of excitement and awe at that initial sight from the architect's windows.

The Windfall

My job at Pleger and Stevenson continued for about ten weeks until a stroke of good luck freed me from my low-self-esteem job in early spring. Two years before my *jackpot job*, I had been employed as a concessionaire for one dollar per hour, tax free, at the bustling Buffalo Zoo. While working there, I met an entirely new group of people, all of whom came from better financial circumstances than I. The vast majority of these young men came from families with professional or white-collar fathers. All of those forty or so kids (mostly under eighteen years of age) were college bound with the expectation of prosperity and success. The formula was simple: do well in high school, go to college, achieve good grades, and then get a lucrative professional job. All my fellow workers exuded an assumption of prosperity and a sense of future good fortune.

I thought, *Hey, I'm a good student, and I work as hard or harder than most of these kids—why can't I be as successful?* What I didn't understand at the time was that my work motivation was a galaxy away from theirs. Those kids worked for spending money, clothes money, and savings account money. I, on the other hand, worked in part for clothes money and some spending money. Once my father, who was still with our family during my tenure as a concessionaire at the Buffalo Zoo, got wind of how much I earned during the summer school recess period between June and September, he craftily got me to "contribute" most of my pay to the family income. I felt somewhat cheated but was uncertain as to the reason for this feeling.

Had my father, who had been working as a bartender since 1960, been as dedicated to our family as I was, I would've felt my contribution was the right thing to do. However, my earnings were not adding to our family income. Instead, they allowed my father to keep more of his bartending earnings to use as cabaret money to entertain his friends or his mistress, who gave birth to their first illegitimate child in January 1961. I had unwittingly helped enable my father to cultivate a relationship that would eventually sabotage our family bond.

Around the time of Pope John XXIII's death in June 1963, in my second year at the zoo, while washing out five-gallon glass jugs used for orange and grape drink, I severely sliced my right thumb at its base. The large bottle that I was washing was wet and slippery, and it unexpectedly jumped from my hands. As I attempted to recover my grasp, the bottom of the bottle met the hard sink. My hand had begun to clutch the neck of the bottle just as it began to shatter. Instead of grabbing the top of the bottle, my hand disappeared into giant shards of razor-sharp glass, which effortlessly slashed the base of my right thumb in a crescent moon pattern. Blood flowed over the broken glass, and my employer, Jimmie B., almost instantly appeared. He led me to his car and sped off. His frantic screaming cleared our way into the emergency room of Sisters Hospital. I remained calm and focused while Jimmie yelled at everyone in our path so much that I was certain he would bust his aorta. Fortunately, that didn't happen, and I was rather quickly cleaned, sutured, bandaged, and returned to work, where I finished my day working with the use of my one good, left hand.

The significance of this accident was that in March 1965, I received an unexpected check from workmen's compensation with a letter stating that my injury sustained at the Buffalo Zoo two years earlier represented a 10 percent loss of the use of my right thumb. The sum I received was equivalent to twelve weeks of gross earnings at Pleger and Stevenson. The check arrived at about the same time the Beach Boys were singing "Help Me Rhonda" and the Hondells were singing about the glories of their Honda motor scooter: "First gear it's all right, second gear I lean right, third gear—hang on tight—faster it's all right." Commercials for the smaller Japanese motorcycles began to appear on television with catchy little tunes. "Solo Suzuki" was sung with images of a young rider gliding along smooth country roads with enchanting, scenic vistas. It was motorcycle karma, and it appealed to my sense of independence and adventure.

One of my friends, Vinnie C., had bought a 55cc Yamaha in Niagara County from a gnarly, old couple who sold motorcycles from their semiconverted barn. We drove to their place on a chilly day in late March. The wind was blowing, and occasionally snow flurries came from the sky like bursts of white confetti. Periodically the sun would slice through the clouds like a prison light frantically searching for escapees. We were approaching the annual transition of seasons, so we welcomed and tolerated this meteorological schizophrenia.

Vinnie introduced me to Walter K. and his wife. It was the first time I had ever seen a man and a woman both wearing blue bib overalls, and, to my amazement, Mrs. K.'s hands had more grease on them than any male mechanic I had ever met. I came to find out that she was a crackerjack mechanic and readily plunged into the greasiest jobs without the slightest thought about the consequences to her once-feminine appendages. They both were down-home people who seemed nice, and I liked them.

I was an easy sell. Once I mounted that little white Yamaha and felt my butt softly on top of the black leather seat built for two, I took possession. It was an instant marriage. Instead of a two-dollar marriage license, I pulled out $295 in small bills in exchange for a bill of sale. One of the younger guys in the showroom/barn (probably a son of the couple) took me out to an adjoining field for a quick, comprehensive driving lesson, which lasted less than ten minutes. I passed it with flying colors since I didn't wipe out or crash into anything. I was able to instantly use the brake, shift gears, and navigate in a straight line. So off I went, maneuvering through the chilly spring air toward my West Side home twenty miles away. I was excited and happy about my acquisition and felt that new adventures lay just ahead.

My work delivering Photostat copies at Pleger and Stevenson had become passé. I had had enough of pedaling in the cold downtown streets and decided that I did not want to tempt fate and be seen by any friends or acquaintances who might skip school and go downtown. I quit my job and immediately abandoned my razor blade. I wanted to grow a full beard as part of my disenfranchisement from the phony world I was rebelling against. With the exception of attending night school (which I enjoyed), I was now a bona fide member of bohemia. The freedom I felt was exhilarating.

In May, a friend of my mother approached me to do a per diem construction job, and I accepted. The job entailed using a pickax and shovel to dig up old abandoned railroad tracks behind a grain mill along the Buffalo River that were to be sold as scrap metal. It was hot, dirty physical work done behind the towering silos of the many grain mills that lined the river like stoic soldiers guarding a fortress in a bygone era. I enjoyed the physical challenge, driving to work on my Yamaha, and not having a supervisor hovering over me like a vulture circling its prey. I could also blast rock music on my transistor radio in the mostly warm May sunlight. It was solitary work, but it suited my purpose at the time.

* * *

CHAPTER TWO

≟

Two Worlds Meet

Throughout the early spring, I continued to attend night school and socialize with my friends. We went to the dance at Mount Major on Friday nights. It was kind of an holy day of obligation where we could hear local bands do their damnedest to sound like the icons of our music, especially the Beatles, the Rolling Stones, and even the Kingsmen ("Louie, Louie"). But, more importantly, it was a place to see and meet new girls. Following the dance, which ended at eleven p.m., most of the guys would walk a short city block to a little gin mill called the Char-Pit. It was famous for great steak sandwiches served on French bread, with hot peppers on the side, for half a buck. More importantly, a glass of draft beer was only fifteen cents. For two dollars you got fed and got a good beer buzz. What a deal!

The Char-Pit was also famous for ignoring the liquor laws and serving minors or just about anyone who could fork over the price of a beer. I had a particular advantage over my friends and high school frat brothers: my father, a.k.a. Nick Ferocious, was the bartender and manager overseeing the hedonistic teenage festivities. Almost every guy in the bar was there because he wanted to eat, drink, and shoot the breeze about our little but active world on the west side of town. It was always an obligatory schedule we followed, unless we got lucky and met a hot babe or were invited to a party somewhere else. Since most parties were on Saturday nights, we almost always ended up at the Char-Pit on Fridays, and we *never* came with females. It was an unwritten rule that if a female was present, barroom male behavior had to be repressed.

Guys went to the Char-Pit to unleash outrageous behavior, not to act too civilized.

On Friday, May 28, 1965, the Memorial Day weekend, I followed my usual routine of going to Mount Major to hang out with my Kappa Phi frat brothers and associated friends. The music was by the inimitable derivative band called the Buffalo Beatles. They could evoke a Beatle-like sound with their rendition of our idols' music. It was close enough, and we danced and talked and wandered about the floor looking for new faces—or faces that had struck a note in our hearts on another occasion. Outside of a rare fight, which was quickly broken up by bouncers or the guard who stood vigilantly by the entrance, the night was predictable. Afterward, we knew it was off to the Char-Pit and, if any money was left after that, to the Your Host Restaurant in the West Side Plaza. Their coffee was fifteen cents, and French fries with gooey gravy was another two bits (twenty-five cents).

On that particular night, I was hanging out with my buddy Butch. Our friendship seemed to reignite every two years, and we had walked the same path the past winter as recent high school dropouts. The script for the night began the same as so many other times. The music was loud enough to thwart our ability to differentiate it from the original versions. We heard what we wanted; it suggested the real thing, and, for us, it became the real thing. It made us feel good and helped us to be released from our personal inhibitions.

We scanned the swirling crowd to see familiar faces and to spot new faces, attractive faces, faces with possibility. It was natural selection in its primordial glory. Sometimes you'd see someone appealing, but they would have a girlfriend with them who wasn't attractive. The unspoken rule was that if you were with a buddy, you had to find someone attractive not only for yourself but for your friend as well. When there were two guys, you had to find two decent-looking girls. We hunted in pairs.

Well she looked at me, and I, I could see
That before too long I'd fall in love with her ...
From: "I Saw Her Standing There" by The Beatles

On this particular Friday night, before a long holiday weekend that energized us with an especially carefree attitude, we saw two new faces not far from the entrance to this teen paradise. We cut a path straight to them to initiate the introduction phase. "Hi, where are you from?" "We've never seen you before." "This band is great, isn't it?" "Want to dance?"

The dancing part was my greatest hurdle. I could get by, but my forte wasn't dancing. I had a passion for living and loved to converse about anything and everything with anyone. So after the requisite dance, I began talking with one of the young ladies, who, I discovered, was a senior at South Park High School. She was an honors student, no less, who had a fondness for poetry and folk music. I immediately sensed a faint but distinct intellectual echo. We became drawn into a conversation, which went from instant rapport to something else, something beyond teenage small talk. I can't speak for her, but I felt electricity traveling through me. I sensed a force unlike any other I had ever felt in my life. Just seventeen, a high school dropout, a recent survivor of my family's painful schism, I could feel a greatness, a powerful, positive force touching my very core at that moment.

Our intriguing conversation was prematurely cut short by the bus schedule. Marilyn and her best friend, Olga, had to catch the first of the two buses to get them home on the other side of town. Marilyn gave me her telephone number before she left, and I promised to call her. We watched them enter their first bus in front of Mount Major on West Ferry Street and then vanish from sight. In my adolescent life, I had gone through this simple ritual of receiving a phone number on a slip of paper many times, most often forgetting to follow up, or misplacing the piece of paper and never making contact. When I actually called someone's number, I almost always found that the subsequent conversation, with no music drowning out every other word, paled in comparison to my initial contact. Once the naked intellect and verbal skills were exposed, my interest decreased proportionally.

During one of those telephone conversations, a short-term girlfriend (her name was Rosie S.) began telling me about her favorite new song, "The Name Game" by Shirley Ellis. She began singing the lyrics: "Shirley!/ Shirley, Shirley, bo-birley, banana fanna fo firley/ Fee fy mo Mirley, Shirley! ..." When I realized she was going to sing the whole damn song, I placed the telephone receiver down, went to the bathroom to answer nature's call, came back, and picked up the receiver. Rosie was still singing "The Name Game." Needless to say, that relationship went nowhere. The only reason I even pursued it was that her best friend, Bonnie, was dating my frat brother, Hawk, and I thought it would be cool if we had best friend girlfriends.

But Marilyn S. was different than any other young woman I had ever met before. She had somehow transcended the world she was born into, and I recognized through some internal and mysterious alchemy that I must reconnect with her. I scrupulously inserted the piece of paper with her name and phone number into my wallet. The sound of her voice seemed to reverberate in my ears; her words about poetry electrically charged my mind. There was no doubt she was someone special and significant.

That night I dreamt I was wandering through a flower-filled garden and ran into Marilyn, who was lost and asked for my help. We walked and walked, never seeing another person, and then sat by a pond and ate fresh fruit that we had picked from nearby trees. When we realized there were no other people anywhere, we held hands, embraced, and kissed passionately. At that point in the dream, the morning sunlight coming through my bedroom window awoke me. I felt as if something great was on the horizon, and my mood was incredibly upbeat.

Beer-Blast at the Lake

In the early afternoon the next day (Saturday), I crossed paths with one of my few friends who owned his own motorcycle, Lenny I., and he invited me to go with him to a beer-blast thirty miles southwest of Buffalo in a place called Point Breeze. It was a famous place for teen partying. A few years earlier it was *the* place to go to, but it had been targeted by law enforcement. Summer teen partying began to drift northward into Canada to Sherkston Beach, Crystal Beach, and Bay Beach. The glory days of the early 1960s at Point Breeze were fading, but there were occasional parties that rivaled its heydays.

Lenny I. was an amazing person. He was a gifted athlete with a terrific physique who had attained legendary status by gaining over a hundred yards rushing in a junior varsity football game for his Catholic high school team in a single game, part of which was done on a fractured leg. He was 5'7" tall and weighed about 180 pounds: all muscle. But Lenny, despite his remarkable athletic prowess, was just a regular guy interested in all the usual stuff we mere mortals liked.

He owned an 80cc Yamaha motorcycle and drove it like a man possessed. My smaller bike struggled to keep up with him. Lenny had once sped through the famous S turns on Hertel Avenue in North Buffalo at about forty-five miles per hour. If that doesn't sound very daring, consider that he did it with both his arms folded across his chest. He was able to lock the throttle of his motorcycle to maintain his speed, nonchalantly fold his arms across his chest, and use body English to maneuver his speeding motorcycle through the winding street.

We drove to Point Breeze on the Saturday afternoon of the long weekend. The weather was warm and clear, and traffic remained relatively light. Lenny had heard about a beer-blast that was going to take place on Sunday afternoon from one of his many contacts. The question of where we could stay the Saturday night before the actual beer-blast the next day was no issue at all for Lenny. Among his other attributes, Lenny was a great improviser. We went to the beach, met some other young people, caught some rays, ate at an inexpensive greasy spoon restaurant, and proceeded to a highly secluded summer cottage with some of the new people we had met that very day.

Once we entered the cottage, we could see candles on the table for lighting. There was no electricity, and we were made aware that our newfound friends were neither the owners of the cottage nor related to them. In fact, the cottage had been randomly opened and used by squatters. Nothing was damaged or removed. The petite dwelling was being used just as a place to sleep. Why this particular cottage had been opened no one could say; perhaps, I surmised, because it was so well hidden.

A Factory Worker's Shangri-la

Point Breeze was a summer destination, mostly for blue-collar Buffalonian families who purchased or built these minimalist dwellings. They often consisted of two or three compact bedrooms with a small bathroom (or an outhouse) and a combination living room, kitchen, and dining room. They usually were on small plots of land, and privacy was a necessary casualty of this affordable formula. You could see cottage after cottage after cottage along every road as you moved away from the public beach. Many roads weren't even paved, and sidewalks were not even an afterthought. It would've been like expecting a glass of fine Merlot with your Happy Meal at McDonald's. It was an utterly ridiculous notion.

These were the very minimal-cost structures, haphazardly furnished, that allowed thousands of working class families to escape their urban confinement for ten weeks of prime summer along the extensive Lake Erie shoreline. Just being by the water, away from the stench of the industrial juggernauts that employed most of the vacationers, was uplifting. Tens of thousands worked at Bethlehem Steel, Republic Steel, National Analine, Ford Stamping Plant, or General Motors facilities and earned what was considered a good wage, enough to afford the luxury of a cottage along the shores of Lake Erie southwest of Buffalo or across the US-Canadian border in Crystal Beach or Bay Beach.

After a guilt-laced night in our free accommodation, we went on to attend our Sunday afternoon outdoor beer-blast. For a couple of bucks you received a glass and an open invitation to visit the beer keg as often as your young bladder could tolerate. After six rather rapid visits to the silver orb, the world became simple, uncomplicated, and fun. My spirit was set free to soar above its earthly limitations, or so it seemed. Laughter replaced words, and all defenses melted away. It was artificially induced nirvana. Everything became transparent and beautiful. The reel of laughter drowned out the poor-quality sound of the hi-fi music playing in the background of this open-air celebration. Time passed quickly, and the gathering began to shrink as the keg gasped out its last remaining drops of hop-filled magic elixir. Once the beer in the keg was gone, we realized it was time to go home.

Ride Back to Reality

Lenny and I headed toward our trusted Japanese steeds to begin our ride back to reality—our city lives. We were not sober, but we were coherent and coordinated enough to operate our two-wheel chariots. We had managed to budget our money in such a way as to be completely broke by the end of our fun-filled weekend on the lake. The money was gone, and our return home was an unwanted necessity.

Off we zoomed, Lenny flying ahead with me hot on his trail. Route 5 was a fast, direct way back to Buffalo. Lenny was feeling infallible and began to turn our straight, boring ride home into an adventure. At one point, he dropped back behind me. After a couple of seconds, he came roaring past me with his arms comfortably folded across his chest, performing his trademark maneuver until I no longer could see him around another curve in the road.

I throttled as hard as I could to get my little Yamaha to its maximum speed of 58–60 miles per hour (depending on the wind velocity and incline of the road). Suddenly, as I wound around the curve, I saw Lenny on the side of the road, his bike up on its kickstand. He was sitting in an upright position with his hands on the ground behind him. I quickly exited onto the shoulder of the road and drove up to him to see what was wrong.

"Is there anything wrong, Len?"

He replied, "Na, I was taking a break until you caught up." Then he jumped up, hopped on his cycle, and blasted off, continuing our journey back home with me pushing my little Yamaha to its maximum speed once again.

Because of this accelerated pace, two unforeseen things happened. Outside a snooty suburb called Wanakah, my little machine began to overheat. Overheating usually caused the single spark plug to get fouled-out with carbon and unable to fire properly. My intrepid motorcycle started to sputter and cough and then gasped out "I quit" as the engine stalled out. I coasted off the road onto the gravel shoulder. As luck would have it, there was no gas station or house in sight.

Lenny, realizing I was not behind him, circled back to where I was parked. After I told him what was wrong, we both knew what needed to be done to get back on the road. My little motor was overheated, and the lone spark plug was coated with a layer of thick, black carbon that must be removed before the engine would start. Our choices were few. We could allow the engine to cool on its own in the late spring sun, or we could expedite the process by dumping water on it. It had to be cooled before our hands could get near the spark plug housed in the molten hot piston.

There was a drainage ditch nearby, so we found an empty, discarded paper coffee cup and headed down into the ditch to find a pocket of water. *Drat!* It was completely dried up. But after a second of serious deliberation, we unzipped the fronts of our jean shorts and began to use our natural resource to do the deed. The motor made a sizzling sound as it converted our recycled beer into a pungent steam that vanished into the warm midafternoon sunlight.

After the success of phase one of the repair job, it was a simple matter of taking the spark plug out of its housing with my little tool set that fit nicely in its special compartment under the leather seat. Having been through this process on a number of occasions, I had enclosed a piece of sandpaper with my tool kit to sand off the electrode and metal areas around the spark plug. This needed to be done to allow the spark plug to fire properly.

Once this was accomplished, I reinserted the cleaned spark plug and kick-started my mechanical *Rocinante*. It started with no extra effort, and, once again, we resumed our homeward trip. Everything seemed fine and dandy for about ten more miles until, again, my motorcycle unexpectedly started sputtering. But this time it had nothing to do with the spark plug. I had simply run out of gas.

How could this happen? The 55cc Yamaha was a marvel of technology in a lot of ways. However, it had some major shortcomings, one of which was that it did not have a gasoline gauge. And being a two-stroke or two-cycle engine, it required motor oil to be mixed directly with the gasoline in the fuel tank. My model preceded the so-called *auto-lube* innovation, which automatically injected the right proportion of oil with the fuel.

So now Lenny and I found ourselves in Lackawanna, just southwest of Buffalo, out of gasoline, out of oil, out of money, and with yet another dilemma. My cashless wallet, which I exclusively used to store my license and registration, was missing from my rear pocket. Those were the days before credit cards, so that little annoyance wasn't really a significant part of the equation, nor was it a reason for great alarm at the moment.

Lackawanna, in those days, was the home of bustling Bethlehem Steel Mill, which employed upward of twenty thousand workers in one of America's oldest, least efficient, dirtiest steel producing facilities. The stench and omnipresent floating, flickering dust permeated the entire city of Lackawanna, and when the westerly winds picked up, the city of Buffalo was reminded by the pungent odor that a big, filthy business was in full-throttle mode nearby. At night, when pig iron was poured into Lake Erie, a red glow was projected into the sky that was visible from the city and was often the basis for children's ghost stories. It was said that if you needed fresh air in Lackawanna, you had to go into your basement. It was also said that birds living in Lackawanna didn't chirp but instead coughed in the film-covered trees that survived in the rust-colored smoke spewing from the numerous industrial smokestacks.

There we were, just as the work shift was changing, flat broke and wondering what we were going to do next. Then, amazingly, I noticed a familiar figure in the horde of men marching dejectedly like a prison chain gang toward the plant entrance at Gate 3. It was none other than my brother-in-law, Sam, going into work on the second shift. I quickly got his attention and explained my predicament to him. He generously loaned me two bucks, enough to fill my three-gallon tank and buy a quart of oil to finish the process of refueling.

I thanked him, and Lenny and I walked down the street to a gas station. We filled my gas tank, poured in the calculated proportion of motor oil, closed the gas cap, and shook my motorcycle like a giant milkshake. Once again, I kick-started my valiant Yamaha, and it sang out its trademark rapid high-pitched sound: *"Ra,ra,ra,ra!"* Off we went the final few miles to our respective homes. Once we reached the downtown city limit, Lenny headed east to his Cleveland Hill–area, owner-occupied neighborhood, while I went back to the West Side of Buffalo and my mother's rented flat.

* * *

CHAPTER THREE

Chance Encounter

A few days later, with no notion of what had happened to my wallet, I attended night school. When I reflect back, I have no idea why I wasn't the least bit alarmed by my lost wallet and had no sense of urgency to replace my missing documents. I pushed it to the back of my mind and trudged on as if nothing had happened to my license and registration. But I was upset by one aspect of my lost wallet. In one of the inner pockets was a slip of paper containing the name "Marilyn S." and her telephone number. What could I do? How would I ever call her to continue our intriguing conversation? As if by some divine intuition, I left the question alone, feeling an answer would be forthcoming by some mysterious means. Exactly what that was, I had no clue. But I felt it deep inside of me nonetheless.

This was not the reaction of a mature adult, who would've justifiably fretted and frowned and gone through needless anxiety without ever reaching a solution. My naïveté and *premature* attitude was a far more simplistic approach, which, in the end, was preferable to pulling one's hair, wringing one's hands, or cursing in frustration. There was a powerful feeling within me that made me confident things would somehow work out.

On the following Friday, I spoke to my friend Butch, who was still working in the downtown Buffalo area at his uncle's gas station, and made plans to have lunch together. Getting about on the crowded and congested streets was easy with my little Yamaha, and parking was a snap. Just jump a curb and pull into any sliver of space three feet by six feet. It was Friday, June 4, 1965, a clear, warm, beautiful, sunny spring afternoon. Butch was on the back of my motorcycle as I drove north up Main Street after a quick, cheap lunch at America's Best Texas Redhots on Washington Street. It was a restaurant my father had introduced me to several years earlier on one of those rare occasions when he took me out to eat without our entire family clan.

Butch and I had eaten fast, talked fast, and burned up most of his scanty hour break. Afterward, we drove up Main Street so we could watch people as we traveled toward East Tupper Street and his uncle's gas station. All of a sudden, I caught sight of two blonde teenage girls coming out of L.L. Berger's, a high-quality ladies' clothing store. To my utter amazement, one of the two young women was none other than the owner of the missing telephone number safely stored in my lost wallet. In fact, it was Marilyn with her friend Olga, the very same two girls from the previous Friday night at Mount Major.

I made a beeline toward them, illegally U-turned, and stopped by the curb in front of them, which caught them by surprise. I immediately explained to Marilyn why I hadn't called her, and she seemed fine with my sincere and truthful excuse. Then, frantically, we began our conversation, trying to pick up from our first meeting at the dance exactly one week earlier. I looked at both young women in the penetrating sunlight and thought to myself how lovely and attractive each was and how they both appealed to me. But there was something incredibly rare and extra special about Marilyn, something I could not resist and something my innermost being wanted to touch, to connect with. The power of this attraction would be unequaled in my entire life. Somehow I knew this at that moment.

We made small talk at first. The girls had the afternoon off from school after taking one of their New York State Regents Exams that morning and were doing a little celebratory shopping, we found out. Then, in a bold move, I asked Marilyn if she would like to go for a ride out to the lake that very night. It was sunny and warm, and we could count on a typically magnificent sunset by the water off Point Breeze. To my complete and utter amazement, she agreed and gave me specific instructions on how to get to her South Buffalo street corner. Six p.m. was our rendezvous time, and I cannot articulate how excited and amazed I was to have had this chance encounter with the special person whose phone number was concealed in the pocket of my missing wallet. I accepted this miraculous encounter as a sign this was meant to be—it was kismet.

Although the girls had time to talk to us, it now was Butch and I who were in a hurry. His uncle was a self-made small businessman who would not tolerate tardiness, laziness, or anything less than complete commitment to a full-time, minimum wage job. So, reluctantly, we once again said good-bye and parted. But unlike a week earlier, when I had been given a telephone number and had only a vague hope of something in the future, I now had a definite date for that very day—just five hours away at six p.m. I dropped Butch off at his uncle's gas station and made my way back to my West Side home in anticipation of a glorious night. There was a stream of titillation rapidly and repeatedly flowing through my spirit. Something great was on the horizon; I knew it and could feel it with complete certainty. Like a religious pilgrim, I believed I was about to be touched by a force far more powerful than anything I had ever experienced.

The Highest High

Everybody's got to love somebody sometime
Everybody's got to win a heart
Everybody's got to love somebody sometime
When you do, I hope you never part ...
From: "Listen People" by Herman's Hermits

Later that afternoon, after meticulous steps to prepare myself, I went through a mental checklist to assure myself that nothing would go wrong. On the way home from our chance encounter, I had stopped at a gas station close to home to top off my gas tank, essentially replacing all the fuel I had used since running out of gas in Lackawanna five days earlier. I was now wearing one of my favorite, genuine bleeding madras shirts (under my white cable-knit, V-neck tennis sweater), white jeans, and my prize pair of real British Walker shoes, and I was lightly splashed with English Leather cologne.

As I critically peered into the full-length mirror in front of me, I was pleased with my image. Although my youthful full beard was not as dense as a mature man's, it was the perfect rebellious statement I wanted to project. It separated me from my friends and gave me a sense of uniqueness. My hair was longer than that of most of my friends, who were still in high school and restricted by a rigid dress code. The person staring back at me was intense and generally misunderstood or underestimated by those whom he encountered. People either liked me a lot or didn't, but all saw me as a rebel. I always remained true to myself and never tried to be anything other than what my inner voice dictated. I would come to learn the term "inner-directed," which would somewhat sum up my basic demeanor.

Marilyn thought that her parents might object to my rather rebellious appearance, so I was to meet her on her street corner, which was about seventy-five yards from her house and out of visual sight of where we met. Her parents were older and more conservative than my mother. The South Buffalo neighborhood they lived in was working class with primarily one-family dwellings with modest yards and few garages. Her neighborhood was new to me since I had no friends or relatives living there. But if people were nice and respectful toward me, I could get along with anyone. I had no prejudices or biases whatsoever. Good people were good people in my mind.

My ride to our meeting place was filled with excitement and a young man's angst. I began to have second thoughts and doubts about this hastily arranged date. Was I deluding myself like with Rosie S., who sang "The Name Game" over the telephone? Or would this be something truly different than anything I had ever experienced? Were my expectations so lofty that I would be doomed to disappointment? Up to that point in my life, I had always remained optimistic, although most of my experiences should have challenged my will and ability to remain open to new ones. After being hurt by someone or something in life, we often withdraw into a safe, protected place within ourselves. And as this keeps us somewhat protected from negative outside forces, it locks out the possibility for new and exciting adventures. I eagerly chose to leap into the unknown and see what might happen.

The natural force within me, driving my spirit toward that meeting place, was as powerful as any force in my nature. I had to get there, couldn't wait to get there, must get there—and not a moment late. I arrived at the designated corner of G. Street and Seneca Street at the precise prearranged time. No sooner had I arrived when I caught sight of Marilyn walking purposefully toward me. She was wearing white hip-hugger bellbottom pants with a blue and white horizontally striped boatneck shirt and lace-up brown sandals. Her hair was long and blonde like spun, thick strands of living gold and was specially woven into one braid down the center of her back. Her blue eyes were two beacons that penetrated the deepest part of my soul. The image of her beautiful smile that evening haunts me to this day. No great painter could capture on canvas any smile more beautiful and powerful than the one left in my mind by her at the moment she approached me on the street corner that night.

We quickly kissed, and she mounted the back of the double seat of my humble white Yamaha. In an instant, we were off toward the lake and an evening of getting to know one another and testing the apparent magical power of our new acquaintance—or else singing a hearty version of "The Name Game." It seemed that fate had brought us together and then reacquainted us and now was facilitating our first date.

I felt her arms around me, and it felt as if our bodies had fused together. Her perfect form pressed against my back, and my heart raced wildly. The scent of her perfume filled my head with images of beauty and unleashed a rush of unparalleled optimism. I felt as if we were floating through air instead of gliding along the road on a mortal Yamaha motorcycle.

We drove down Old Lake Shore Road, passing Darwin Martin's Frank Lloyd Wright–designed Graycliff House along the way to Point Breeze. It was a place I had visited with other young women with whom I almost never was able to connect in both a physical and an intellectual way. That quaint little town along the lake had a certain special meaning for me because I had made a breakthrough connection there with an attractive, bright, teenage woman the previous year, in August, at about the time my parents' marriage and our family were going through the final stage of dissolution.

Infamous Hillary L. would always represent for me the flip side of beauty and trust. She would come to characterize the treachery that sometimes lurked behind physical beauty. Hillary took me into her confidence, connected with me in a cerebral way beyond teenage dialogue and our tender age. But when I dropped all my defenses, she turned around and went off with one of my new friends. It crushed me terribly and became the theme of my first, albeit lugubrious, poem,

"The Agony in the Rain" ("You ran off with my new friend/And this my darling was the end").

Marilyn and I arrived in time to park the motorcycle, take the blanket I brought with us, and walk past the public area to a secluded cove around the north end of the beach. The water temperature was still in the upper fifties, and it was chilly by the shoreline, so I gathered driftwood and started a small fire. We relaxed on the old blanket spread over the pebble and sand beach facing the water and the sun in the western sky.

We began talking about the natural beauty in front of us and then started exploring everything we found interesting. We discussed the new topical folk music phenomenon that was shining a critical light on the social and political issues of our time. We spoke about the civil rights movement and the injustices in the world. We talked about the genius of Bob Dylan and the haunting music of Joan Baez. Marilyn and I shared a love for Buffy Sainte-Marie, Simon and Garfunkel, Peter, Paul, and Mary, Pete Seeger, and all folk music in general. And we both loved and listened to the phenomenal canon of British Invasion music from the Beatles, the Rolling Stones, Zombies, Herman's Hermits, Manfred Mann, Gerry and the Pacemakers, the Kinks, and virtually scores of others.

We spoke about poetry and the power of language. Marilyn had been exposed to the works of many great poets, among others Robert Graves, in her honors English class. It would be many years later that Robert Graves, one of the great, prolific love poets of the twentieth century and a literary lion of letters, would become a significant part of my life and I would be a guest of his widow in Deia, Mallorca, on many visits after his death in 1985. But his name was first brought to my attention by Marilyn in the romantic rustic cove in the golden glow of sunset on our first date.

She was a child and I was a child,
In this kingdom by the sea,
But we loved with a love that was more than love
I and my Annabel Lee—
With a love that the wingéd seraphs of Heaven
Coveted her and me.
From: "Annabel Lee" by Edgar Allen Poe

My exposure and taste in poetry was, and would always be, quite eclectic. I had been deeply affected by Edgar Allen Poe's writings, especially "Annabel Lee," a poignant gothic love poem that recounts an all-encompassing possessive and pervasive love for his real-life young wife, who tragically died from consumption. I had identified with it largely because I was young and passionate and inherently felt it to be a vision of love that would someday touch my life. The intensity of Poe's love, his commitment to his beloved Annabel Lee, and the profound loss he experienced after she was taken from him resonated in my growing, pure, innocent consciousness.

The depth of that love is what I longed for, and my search, remarkably, started when I read that poem in grade school. Poe's poem was a revelation, giving words and vision to what I felt deep within me. Falling in love with someone was one thing, but finding someone who returned the same degree of love and passion was quite another.

There were many times when I felt the rumbling of emotion, and it usually followed a familiar pattern. A physical attraction started the process with its immediate raised level of expectation. That was the easy part, and many beautiful teenage women provided the spark. But the second part of the process was the rub and always dashed my eager spirit and hungering heart. Getting past the physical realm and exploring the mind of an appealing, attractive young beauty had always ended in either outright disappointment or in a slight bubble of hope that soon popped and vanished. All my relationships had left me with a sense of sadness for the women involved and for myself. I felt sad for them because I imagined that they might never feel the full force of passion and power associated with a love equally driven by physical love and intellectual awareness. I felt sadness for myself because I was anxious about having to wait more time for what I was certain was my destiny.

Poe's words echoed in my mind and heart like an endless anthem, an endless quest for my one, true love: *"She was a child and I was a child/In this kingdom by the sea/But we loved with a love that was more than love ..."* Achieving *that* intensity of love in a full and complete relationship had become the silent guiding force within me. I felt as though I must reach for the stars to attain heaven. Many false starts had been made, but my indefatigable, youthful optimism kept driving me.

Many of my friends and peers settled for convenient relationships that involved brief passion and much banality. Some friends dated girlfriends for years and years and seemed almost to be monotonously married. Nearly every one of them complained about their girlfriends and lustfully looked at other girls. Others bounced from one casual liaison to another with carnal conquest as the sole objective. Neither extreme held great appeal for me, although the latter was most often the result of my youthful encounters. My search for a kindred spirit of the opposite sex was my overriding motivation; I had reached a plateau of consciousness beyond my friends. There was a torrid fire of physical attraction, but it was always coupled with a passion for intellectuality that sought to continually reexamine and redefine my boundaries of self-awareness. My mind was growing, and I could feel the pure power of my evolving intellectuality in ways that made me excited and confident beyond my impoverished circumstances.

Part of this cognitive energy was used to entertain those around me. I could make people laugh with my wild, creative imagination and free-spirited nature, and I often did. But my need to connect on an intellectual plane grew. I didn't want to just make people laugh; I wanted to find a woman with whom I could explore the serious questions and observations entering my exponentially growing mind. I felt an awesome power within and realized that much of what I thought could not be discussed with most of my friends. Higher education would feed this inner fire and be a part of my future, but I needed a woman to share with me the joy of intellectual curiosity and revelation. I found myself intensely looking for a kindred spirit who was driven by the same thirst and amazement for art, for literature, for poetry, for the world, and for all learning as I.

> *I saw the best minds of my generation destroyed by madness,*
> *starving hysterical naked,*
> *dragging themselves through the negro streets at dawn looking for*
> *an angry fix,*
> *angelheaded hipsters burning for the ancient heavenly connection*
> *to the starry dynamo in the machinery of night,*
> *who poverty and tatters and hollow-eyed and high sat up smoking*
> *in the supernatural darkness of cold-water flats floating*
> *across the tops of cities contemplating jazz ...*
> From: *Howl* by Allen Ginsberg

I felt the exciting power of thoughts and ideas circulating through my unbridled mind. At times, I was unable to handle the conscious flow of so many thoughts. On one occasion, I remember finding a book of Allen Ginsberg's poetry in, of all places, a pool hall. This particular collection included his seminal poem *Howl*, which I read with sheer amazement. I was dumbfounded by the power of the searing, passionate images of alienation and frustration. No one I knew at the time was aware of this poet and his work, nor should they have been since most were still in rather typical high schools with restricted curriculums. But I instantly felt that Ginsberg and his words would impact my life in some way. What I didn't know then was that I would meet many great poets, including Allen Ginsberg, and be involved with one of the great collections of original manuscripts and first editions of British and American authors. I would make important connections that would lead me to visit and work with Beryl Graves, the widow of Robert Graves, in Deia, Mallorca. But in 1965, as a high school dropout, I hadn't even dreamt of such a prospect.

The power of poetry captured my expanding mind with its highly compressed language and symbolism and seemed the perfect vehicle for expression. In grade school and high school, I had been exposed to a wide variety of styles, which gave me an appreciation for diversity and an admiration for precise language. Like other inquisitive students, I experimented with writing poetry and achieved modest results. But the exercise was a great cleansing process that would heighten my respect and reverence for language.

But still, I was a healthy male teenager with the same powerful physical urgencies as my peers. That part of my life kept me grounded and connected to my friends. We shared and reveled in our maturing physicality. It was inescapable and inevitable. Where our lives would go on the wave carrying us was unknown. We simply embraced the common joy of our emerging manhood. Every day was exciting and mysterious, and we awoke in the morning eager for what might come.

Unlike any of my friends or acquaintances, Marilyn was perfectly in tune with me. She was both intellectually curious and physically passionate—just like me. We were two similar energy forces seemingly brought together by fate, and together we merged into a greater force. There was no doubt in my mind that this enchanting woman was meant to be my muse and soul mate. Before we left the beach that night, I came to believe that she was the reason I had been born. She had empowered me with a joy and love that I had never known and which would never be equaled again in my life. I fell in love with her: first with her physical beauty and then with her dazzling, young mind.

We spoke for hours, going from subject to subject, in a celebration of free-form discourse as we lay reclined on the old blanket in the hidden cove. We sensed that the conversation, which went back and forth from her to me, had a seemingly endless impetus. We both recognized the enormity of the time we were sharing. And during our wondrous conversation, we held and kissed. I found myself wanting to be close to her, feeling her arms around me, kissing her supple, sensuous lips and gazing into those extraordinary, eternally blue eyes. The force of what I felt was terrifying, as if I were falling off a steep cliff. It scared me to death, but I could not stop. The joy surging through me turned to rapture and propelled me deeper still. Marilyn had become the greatest source of happiness I had ever known. Fate had brought us together, and fate would play out its plan for us. She and I had become *us*. I felt this, I knew this, and I completely surrendered to the fantastic aura enclosing us.

Sunset took place as we kept exchanging our views and opinions about the myriad of subjects that crossed our eager, voracious minds. Both of us continued to respond to the other's comments and the immediate beauty of nature taking place all around us. We listened to the sound of the waves caressing the rocky beach a few yards from our feet, observed the sea gulls soaring past us in hurried flight to get to their nightly retreats and waiting little ones, and, of course, the magnificent crimson sunset as it melted into the water below the western horizon of the surprisingly expansive Lake Erie vista. Once the sun disappeared, the clear, endless sky revealed its billion glittering points of light on the infinite black canvas of night above us. There was magic and electricity in the air.

When sundown pales the sky
I want to hide a while behind your smile
And everywhere I look your eyes I'd find
For me to love you now would be the sweetest thing

It tw'd make me sing
Ah but I may as well try and catch the wind.

At one juncture in our stimulating discussion about the tremendous range of great music of our time, I mentioned to Marilyn another new British singer/songwriter from Scotland. His first American release was a song about love performed in the folk style of Bob Dylan but with a flawless purity that was instantly sensitive and sincere, with no edginess whatsoever. Marilyn had not heard it yet. I pulled out my pocket-sized transistor radio (there was no FM radio in those days) and turned on the great AM rock station WKBW. The first song to be played, and the only song we would listen to that night, was "Catch The Wind" by Donovan—the very song I had just discussed with her. We both intensely listened to the lyrics purely sung by Donovan and immediately realized that this was *our* song and would always be associated with the *us* that had been born that night.

We felt perfectly in tune with nature and with each other. A miracle had just taken place: two people from two radically different backgrounds had merged into a single great consciousness. Intellectually, we had become *one*, and a powerful romantic love had, like a rare and beautiful exotic flower, germinated and bloomed with breathtaking speed. We witnessed this process together, and we both knew that a marriage of true hearts and minds had occurred with staggering quickness.

The sun had set, and the first installment had been made on this momentous promise. Marilyn had to be home by eleven p.m., so it was time to get our blanket folded, put out the fire, and walk back to the place where my motorcycle was parked. As we walked in the deepening darkness across the beach, we held hands tightly. Fearing that this might be a wild, fantastic dream, we squeezed one another's hand with unbelievable firmness as we walked off the peaceful beach. If it was a dream, we did not want it to end. We did not want to let go. Both of us had found our first love, and the euphoria we felt was beyond belief.

Into the Path of a Predator/
The Lowest Low

Once we climbed onto the motorcycle, we set off down Old Lake Shore Road, which was a nicer, more scenic ride than busy and noisy Route 5. After several miles, as the road forked, we went down Bennett Road, which appeared around one of Old Lake Shore's many curves and was yet another alternative to Route 5. Just as we entered Bennett Road, a predominantly residential area, a Honda motorcycle came along going in the same direction. The other rider and I exchanged a couple of comments, as was the custom of bikers of similar type vehicles, and continued driving down the dark, tranquil road.

Up ahead on the left was a popular beach bar for the twenty-something set. When I looked in that direction, I caught sight of a cloud of dust in the dimly lit parking lot and, as we moved toward it, began to hear the sound of rapidly spinning car tires on gravel and dirt. Then, in an instant, I saw the form of a white car bursting through the angry cloud of dust, wildly turning onto our paved road, and madly heading in our direction. Because of the high velocity of the car, its turn onto the road thrust it to our side of the narrow road. All this was happening as we were innocently moving in its direction. We were like sheep walking into the lair of a ravenous wolf.

My reaction was instantaneous: I guided my little white motorcycle to the right, heading onto the minimal shoulder and presumed safety away from this roaring, speeding, almost frothing pallid car. As the front tire of my motorcycle began to touch the dirt and apparent sanctuary of the narrow shoulder area, I could see what was zooming toward us. It was a 1964 Mustang, wearing the cloak of white death. At the instant my front tire touched the shoulder of the road, the left front fender of the meteoric Mustang skimmed past my left knee and leg. My leg was like the cape of a reluctant matador that was taunting a three-thousand-pound albino bull seemingly intent on inflicting great harm.

My precious passenger, now my soul mate and muse, whose trusting arms were wrapped tightly around my waist and unaware of the deadly duel that was occurring, had her head pressed against my back, and her gaze was toward the right side of the road. I felt a split second of relief as I watched the luminous white metal flashing ever so close past my left knee and leg.

Then the front end of my motorcycle lifted skyward like a mushroom cloud after a nuclear detonation. I heard a primal, bloodcurdling scream followed by the unmistakable wailing of pain coming from behind me. The front end of my motorcycle was coaxed down from its nearly ninety-degree apex, and I slammed the brakes on, jumped off, threw the bike up on its kickstand, and rushed toward the source of the terrifying sound.

Marilyn had been hit by the Mustang squarely on her left knee, causing her leg to break and violently pushing her off the motorcycle onto the blacktop road. While I ran toward her, I felt as if I were moving in a surreal dream. I was in shock but didn't know it at the time. Marilyn was on her back squirming in great pain on the road. Her white bellbottoms were now smudged with black from the road, and I could see a growing red stain expanding on her torn left pant leg.

People rushed out of their houses. The other biker, who had witnessed the whole near-death spectacle, stopped to help. The driver of the Mustang turned his car around and actually came back to the scene of the accident. Police were called, an ambulance was summoned, and that quiet, lonely country road was quickly transformed into a carnival of confusion.

A short time later, the ambulance arrived, and Marilyn was placed on a stretcher. I held her hand and told her that I would follow her to the hospital as soon as possible. She said: "Joe, what about your lost wallet? What are you going to do? Are you going to get into any trouble?" She was concerned about my missing wallet, which I had innocently mentioned to her earlier in the day when we met on Main Street outside L.L. Berger's.

"Don't worry. It'll be okay," I said. Then I gently kissed her right cheek as the stretcher was lifted into the back of the anxious ambulance, which promptly drove off with its lights flashing and its siren howling into the tunnel of darkness on its urgent path.

The sheriff's deputy came over to me to get my license and registration and to hear my version of the accident. I reached my hand to my back pocket and then exclaimed: "Oh my God, I must have dropped it on the side of the road! Help me find my wallet!"

A search party was formed, and, of course, nothing was found. The officer was sympathetic, especially after hearing the other motorcyclist verify the details I gave, and after interviewing the obviously intoxicated driver of the white Mustang he allowed me to go. However, I had to leave my Yamaha at the house across the road from the accident scene because I was underage and shouldn't have been driving at night. The legal age to drive at night was eighteen, but, fortunately for me, no summons was issued. My newfound friend on the other motorcycle drove me to Our Lady of Victory (OLV) Hospital in Lackawanna.

I mentioned that I was in a state of shock, but I did not fully comprehend that fact for decades. My erroneous sense of guilt for my part in this near-fatal and tragic event prevented me from ever fully examining the details of that night. I felt an irrational guilt about the accident. In retrospect, we were indeed lucky to have survived, and the drunk driver, whose family had a successful business, would have been thrown in jail and sued for a fortune if the accident had occurred thirty years later. Instead, Marilyn would receive a shameful pittance for her pain and suffering. The scar on her left knee would far outlast the meager compensation she was awarded.

John, my new motorcycle friend, drove me to the hospital, which was some twenty miles away. Thoughts about Marilyn raced through my mind. I could not stop thinking about what happened to her and what she must have been going through each moment since being rushed from the accident scene. In the last few hours, I had experienced the greatest beauty and the greatest tragedy of my brief life. I had reached the peak of my adolescent life and now was descending into the deepest chasm. I went from one to the other in an instant, and I found myself floating in a dreamlike state not fully able to comprehend or believe the events of that wondrous and tragic night.

Fury in a Crowded Corridor

When I arrived at the emergency room, people were scurrying about with precise purpose. It seemed to me that everyone was pitching in to help Marilyn. In reality, there were other people arriving in the emergency room for other emergencies. But in my mind, because I was so focused on Marilyn, an army of staff was assisting her—and only her.

Moments after I arrived, in the midst of observing the frantic movements of the hospital staff, a tall, older, serious woman came slicing through the many moving bodies flowing in the crowded corridor. She approached me, evidently sensing I was a central participant in the whole mess, and said in a focused, pointed, and prosecutorial tone of voice: *"Who was driving the motorcycle?"*

Although Marilyn's mother's question seemed directed at many people, her eyes were locked with fierce precision upon me. I simply acknowledged that I was the driver of the motorcycle. Without an instant's hesitation, she shot back: *"It was your fault!"*

Her indictment of my role, although resolute and swift, was unwarranted given that she had no real knowledge of any actual details other than that a terrible accident had occurred, that her daughter had been injured, and that the long-haired fellow with a beard standing before her was the driver of the motorcycle. She stared hard and deep at me, perhaps waiting for me to confess my guilt in this frightening affair. Behind her, as I learned later, was Marilyn's older brother, Gary, who was on the eve of being shipped to England with the Air Force.

Not one to cower at such a terrible, unjust verbal accusation, I replied with clarity, rational conciseness, and a distinct politeness. I simply pointed out that had her daughter and I been in a car instead of on a motorcycle, we would have been in a head-on collision with the drunk driver of the white Mustang and the consequence would have been far more serious, perhaps even fatal. My stark logic suggested that the motorcycle, in a curious and ironic way, probably saved us from that too-hard-to-imagine outcome. No other barrage of words came my way.

An instant later, the attendants rolled Marilyn by us on a gurney. She had been cleaned and prepped for surgery and was beneath a crisp white sheet the color of a pure cumulus cloud. She was calm and sweet and reached her hand out to comfort me. A smile appeared on her face and, like the rays of sunshine after a summer thunderstorm, suggested the welcomed approach of a peaceful calm. She must have surmised that her mother's wrath had been unleashed and I needed to be reassured and comforted. "Are you all right? Did the sheriff's deputy give you a hard time about your lost wallet?" she said with genuine concern about the trouble I might have gotten into.

We continued to hold hands as I said, "It was okay; don't give it another thought." Just as fast as the gurney had appeared, it was whisked away to a hidden surgical destination.

Marilyn had sustained a broken left leg below the knee, and surgery was necessary to repair it. The events in the emergency room waiting area were a blur after that, and I found myself being driven home to my mother's apartment on Fargo Avenue on the West Side of Buffalo. John, the other motorcycle driver, had been a godsend. I was never to see him after the early morning hours of June 5, 1965, but I could only hope a Good Samaritan played a key role in his life, as he had in mine on that tumultuous night.

Teetotaler's Hangover

When I awoke the next day, it felt as if I had dreamt the sequence of images of the previous twenty-four hours. The parade of memories of the last day spun around in my head like a living Marc Chagall collage: driving downtown with Butch, spotting Marilyn and Olga near L.L. Berger's, riding out to the lake, cuddling on a blanket with a small fire near our feet as we gazed at the emerging stars and moon above the water, driving back home along Old Lake Shore Road, Bennett Road, the crash, the scream, the ambulance, the hospital, and the anger on Marilyn's mother's face. It felt like one of those overwhelming dreams from which you feel great relief after you awaken. But a trip downstairs to the backyard, and my Yamaha's absence from its nighttime parking spot, confirmed my most dreaded fear. It did happen, and it was all terribly true. My life was now upside down and forever changed.

I called the hospital to see how Marilyn was doing and to talk with her. She had gone through surgery and was by herself in a semiprivate room with a cast on her left leg. When I spoke with her, she sounded happy to hear from me. I tried to explain to her my version of what had happened the previous night and to apologize for the terrible outcome. She expressed no anger or regret for going on our first date. Then I told her about my motorcycle being left on Bennett Road in the town of Evans and said that I would have to retrieve it. She was understanding and sweet, and I told her that as soon as I was able to get my Yamaha back, I would visit her at the hospital. She said she understood.

I contacted my friend Lenny to tell him the tale of my last day and to see if he could give me a ride back to the lake to retrieve my motorcycle. He readily agreed to give me a lift back to the accident scene but said it would have to be later in the day. I had no other choice. In those days, teenagers with their own cars were rare. Most depended on their family, friends, or public transportation to get around. Regular public transportation to Evans from Buffalo simply didn't exist back then.

Lenny picked me up later in the day after dinner and drove me back to where my nightmare had begun. I closely inspected my white Yamaha for damage and noticed one, and only one, effect of the terrible accident. The left foot peg, where Marilyn's left foot had been innocently resting, had been bent away from the motorcycle. It was the single, solitary piece of evidence of the force of her left leg being violently thrust backward. The long screw, which went through the center shaft of the foot peg into the motorcycle frame, was bent in a crescent shape. It seemed impossible that with such minor physical damage to the motorcycle, so much pain and suffering could occur.

Night was rapidly approaching by the time we drove out to the lake and inspected my motorcycle. Lenny and I were both tired, him from work and me from emotional overload. I was in no frame of mind to drive home in the darkness, so we needed to find a place to spend the night. We decided to go back to the cottage we had stayed the night before the beer-blast exactly one week earlier. We drove our motorcycles down the same secluded roads, twisting and turning until we came across the same still-vacant cottage with the unlocked door. This time there were no other squatters. Opportunity knocked, and we answered.

Every item in the house was either used or secondhand. No consideration was given to compatibility of color or style. The old kitchen table had four odd chairs that were refugees from different kitchen sets. The curtains all had different and mismatched patterns and were selected for function only. The couch, three chairs, end table, lamps, and rugs showed signs of extensive use but were chosen simply because they were still usable.

There were two single beds, side by side, in one of the bedrooms. Both had their covers disturbed by previous secret visitors. I went back to the bed I had slept in a week earlier when life was so much more innocent and simple. Lenny hopped into the adjoining bed and fell asleep almost straightaway. As I began to relax and to clear my clogged mind as a necessary prelude to a much-needed deep sleep, I found myself trying to smooth over the bedding, which had been made clumpy by an inestimable number of unregistered guests. I straightened out the covers and moved my hand across the bedspread like a rake across a lawn. I felt a bump in the center of the bedding and slid my hand under the covers to see what obstacle was preventing the anxious sleep beckoning me. I grasped the object, which felt rectangular, and then pulled it out.

It was my lost wallet! I instantly opened it and found all the items inside intact: my license, my registration, and a neatly folded piece of paper in one of the pockets. It had remained undisturbed in the bedding for an entire week. I was tremendously relieved to have found it and realized how fortunate I was that the owners of the cottage had not discovered it first and called the police. This was a great break for me, and the enormous relief I felt helped me to enter an intense sleep, which carried me through the night into the morning light.

Shortly after awakening, Lenny and I rode back to Buffalo on our motorcycles with no noteworthy mishaps, detours, or unforeseen calamities. When we reached the city limits, Lenny headed east toward his suburban family home and I headed west to my family's apartment. My mother had been waiting for me to return home to hear the complete painful details of the accident and the aftermath.

My mother was troubled by the news of my accident, and my father, who now openly resided with his mistress and her six children (two of whom he fathered), was sympathetic, although he had no great advice or wisdom to impart upon me. He was not someone to go to for sound, clear advice. His life was basically lived from day to day, with no real consideration for the future. One could never get practical advice from him about dealing with complex issues.

Several days later, I went to see him again at the Char-Pit with a legal document with which I had been served. It named me as a codefendant in a lawsuit resulting from the accident that occurred on Friday, June 4, 1965. Two things stood out as I gazed in shock at the formidable, formal document: my full name, boldly typed across the top, and the mind-boggling sum of $89,000. Considering the average income was about $5,000 per year, I calculated I would have to surrender the equivalent of eighteen years of income to satisfy what this legal instrument was implying. In other words, at the age of seventeen, I was pretty much headed for financial ruin. My youthful ignorance of the legal ramifications of my part in the accident and the insurance industry made for some horrible, sleepless nights and worrisome days.

Once I spoke with my insurance agent and some knowledgeable people, I was made to understand that the financial liability was not going to land on my shoulders but rather on the drunk driver who had nearly claimed the lives of Marilyn and me. It was quite clear from all the information and the testimony of the various parties at the scene of the accident that Marilyn and I were simply innocent victims and all fault was on the head of the drunk driver whose family would ultimately pay.

Visiting an Angel from a Dream

Over the six days after the accident, I traveled to the hospital three times to visit Marilyn. On the first visit to see her, I didn't know whether Marilyn's perception of our time together before the accident was the same as mine. I felt great insecurity about this and began to fear that I may have reinvented the reality of our first date to fulfill my own dream of love.

When I entered her room, which was up on the third floor and had an angular view of the Botanical Gardens building across South Park Avenue, Marilyn was beneath a white sheet, except for her left leg, which was concealed in a sterile white cast on top of the bedding. I could see many unknown autographs scrawled in all directions on the cold, colorless plaster surface. Marilyn gave me a smile that touched my heart. Her hair, blonde and lustrous, hung down on either side of her face, and her eyes, perfectly blue and perfect, penetrated through my anxiousness and welcomed me back to the place where I longed to be. The two female visitors in the room said a quick good-bye and slipped away. I became aware of a mystical process that would happen again and again when we were together. It was one of those proofs that showed whether you were with your soul mate and muse or merely with an ephemeral romantic interest.

When we faced each other and looked deeply into one another's eyes, the outside world seemed to vanish. Nothing existed for me but Marilyn whose eyes were staring hard and deep back at me. The deepest emotion of love I possessed within welled up with such an intensity and surge that I almost felt like screaming aloud with joy. If sadness brings a darkness, then this happiness I felt from my beloved's eyes brought an astonishing lightness, an almost blinding lightness, which instantly vanquished any ills troubling my mind.

The purity and power of the positive emotion created by her intense gazing unleashed the most profound happiness I would ever realize in my life. And I recognized and knew it immediately—we both did. As religious pilgrims refer to the joy and sublime happiness from being touched by God, we felt that type of awareness at the moment our two souls were conjoined in the purest love two people could feel. Ours was "a love that was more than love," and we knew that we must embrace it, hold it, and never let it go. We had become the keepers of a sacred flame that was celebrated by great authors like Shakespeare in his Romeo and Juliet.

We held hands as tightly as we had when we'd left Point Breeze Beach to return to the city on our first night together. We pulled together and kissed with a gentle and holy passion. Without words, beyond words, we knew what had taken place between us and the divine mission that lay before us. The extraordinary communication we would engage in would soon come. The great obstacles attempting to interfere with our sacred journey together would soon appear. But we both knew that we had found our soul mates and that the strength of our new and expanding love would empower us with the courage and tenacity necessary to face any challenge.

I lifted her hand to my mouth and kissed it gently. When I opened my eyes and looked at her, I could see her eyes were glazed over with tears like mine. "Being with you on the beach, in that hidden cove, was the most wonderful experience of my entire life," I said in a soft, passionate whisper.

She looked deeply into my eyes and replied, "Our time together on the beach by the fire was the most beautiful time of my life too." We both instantly felt the same thing and knew its significance.

Then I learned that because of the accident, which would keep

Marilyn in the hospital for nearly a week, she was going to miss the rest of her final New York State Regents Exams and, worse yet, her formal graduation ceremony from high school. She spoke matter-of-factly, with little regret in her voice. This made me feel terrible, and told her so. But Marilyn, in true angelic fashion, assured me that it was no big deal. She would miss one of the important rites of passage, but it didn't matter to her because she knew a greater rite of passage was now taking place. The one was an ending, the other a new, wondrous beginning.

After my third and final visit to the hospital, Marilyn informed me that we would not be permitted to see one another again because of the impending lawsuit. She protested to her parents, but to no avail. Not only were we not supposed to be together but we were not supposed to communicate in any way, either. The formidable obstacles were beginning to appear, and our innocent courage would soon be put to the test. While this stuff began to unfold, I decided I needed to get my life back on a constructive, although predictable, track. My hair was cut and my beard shaved off.

* * *

CHAPTER FOUR

≒

Changing Direction/Walking the Well-Trodden Path

I applied for a job at a supermarket chain called Super Duper and was hired as a stock boy. I also completed my two courses in night school and quickly enrolled in summer school. Marilyn made it clear to me that she wanted to keep our communication alive even though seeing and being together would be impossible in the short term because she would be at home convalescing with her stay-at-home mother close by her side.

We devised an ingenious way to get letters back and forth. Marilyn would have her next-door friend, Kathy M., post her letters to me. My letters to her would be sent to Kathy, who in turn would smuggle them into Marilyn. We also devised a plan to regularly speak on the telephone, which would prove to be the basis for the most comprehensive conversations either of us would ever engage in with another person in our entire lives.

Marilyn's father, Mr. S., was an old railroad engineer for the Norfolk & Western Railroad. He was in his early seventies when Marilyn was seventeen years old. There was a mindboggling two-generation gap between them that made for many contentious arguments. Marilyn's mother was the second Mrs. S. and was much younger than her husband, but older than my parents. The several children from Mr. S.'s first marriage were nearly as old as his second wife. Marilyn's mother was the stereotypical housewife: having and raising children and running the household so as to accommodate Mr. S.'s work schedule.

Although he was old, he worked seven days a week from about six a.m. until noon. He retired to bed every night between nine-thirty and ten p.m. like clockwork. Marilyn's mother faithfully joined her husband as part of her duty to blend into his regimented, highly structured world. This schedule would prove to be our greatest opportunity to continue and expand our communication and relationship.

I attended summer school during the day from Monday through Friday and worked five days a week at Super Duper, most often from around five or six p.m. until ten p.m. I had given Marilyn a series of phone booth telephone numbers, which she would call at the prearranged time of exactly eleven p.m. nightly. My mother had banned me from extensive phone calls at home, and I really didn't want anyone listening in on our extremely private and eventually passionate communication, so I adjusted my activities to accommodate our arrangement. Back in 1965, telephones were actually housed in booths with folding doors. I compiled a list of phone numbers for various booths, which allowed us to have unlimited, free conversations in complete privacy.

During these conversations, we would talk about everything imaginable for as long as we had something worthwhile to say. These conversations quickly evolved into marathon discussions that were some of the most remarkable exchanges I would have with another human being in my life. Nightly, seven days a week without fail, we talked on the telephone from eleven p.m. until four a.m. We never exhausted our conversations or grew tired of one another's voices. Every night turned into the next morning, and we grew deeply sad when it was necessary to hang up the phone. Our conversations eventually began with "I love you" and ended with those same sacred words. When I departed my solitary phone booth, which might be on a street corner, inside an empty twenty-four-hour Laundromat, or perhaps at the old Greyhound bus terminal on Main Street in downtown Buffalo, I felt both exhilarated by our conversation and sad that it had to end until the next night.

I would ride home on my Yamaha motorcycle through the vacant, silent streets, anxious to get a few hours of sleep before beginning my schedule anew so I could be back to my next prearranged spot in time to begin another enchanting conversation with my love, to hear her live voice, to feel her essence envelop me once again. The pure, superlative joy I felt when the sound of her voice reached my ears infused me with an extraordinary courage to face any impediment or challenge. She had redefined what happiness was in my life.

Unlike most relationships, which begin with a physical relationship and then expand into the intellectual realm, our relationship began with intense, comprehensive discussions of all sorts of ideas and a compatible excitement for literature, art, topical protest music, British Invasion music, and current events. Our relationship would only later expand into the physical sphere. We had defied the law of youthful impetuousness for instant physical gratification. We sensed the approach of greatness and accepted the price of biding our time until we could be reunited in one another's arms on our own terms.

Once summer school began, I would be off to a couple of classes followed by an afternoon break before returning to Super Duper. My afternoons were usually spent writing long love letters, touching base with friends, and maybe taking a power nap. My mother had the wisdom and foresight to allow me the freedom to manage my affairs at this transitional and transformational time. I confided in her and explained my feelings and intention to pursue my relationship with Marilyn. My mother could see that ours was no transient teenage love. She trusted me to do the right thing and to steer clear of trouble.

Growing Awareness/ Blossoming Relationship

During the summer of 1965, we were blessed with vibrant, frenetic, incredible music. Even Bob Dylan, the antithesis of melodic, commercial AM radio, managed to surface on the AM band with his "Subterranean Homesick Blues," "Maggie's Farm," and "Like a Rolling Stone." Herman's Hermits, the Kinks, the Rolling Stones, and, of course, the Beatles were everywhere on the airwaves. Certain songs took on special meaning for us and became branded to particular incidents in our lives. Often, the lyrics were thematically parallel to events taking place at the time the songs were being played on the radio. Other songs, which had no thematic connection to what was happening in our lives, would become associated to particular people, places, or memorable events. They became markers in time linked to those things through some sort of intellectual and emotional fusion. Whenever a certain song would be heard, a rush of images and emotions are released into the consciousness. This process persists in my mind to this present day. I can reel off associations of all sorts when I hear those decades-old songs.

When I woke up this morning
You were on my mind
And you were on my mind …
From: "You Were on My Mind" by We Five

When our forced corporeal hiatus began, a song started to be played daily that was a constant reminder of my emotional state. Every weekday morning, as I awoke from my glorified couple-hour nap after my all-night conversation with Marilyn, I would turn on the radio while I began cleaning up for summer school. Without fail, the We Five would be on the air, and their lyrics musically echoed and underlined one of my central thoughts. The song was a constant reminder of my frame of mind and the endless desire I had to be with my Marilyn: *When I woke this morning/You were on my mind*. The words relentlessly pounded in my head and tortured my soul. I had found my soul mate and muse, but I could not be with her. We had been united by fate but separated by circumstances beyond our control. The awesome love and passion we had could only be expressed on the pages of our daily letters and over extensive telephone conversations in the quiescence of the night. While the normal world slept, Marilyn and I exchanged views on every imaginable subject. But most importantly, we exchanged our words of boundless love. The sweetest thing I would ever hear in my life was her pure and beautiful voice telling me: "I love you, Josef."

The only thing that kept me from going mad was the thought that after summer school and my shift at Super Duper, I would be positioned by a predetermined telephone booth with my hand on the receiver, awaiting the phone call from my Venus, my goddess, my love. Every night when the telephone rang, my heart raced, my spirit soared, and I felt truly alive again. It was as if I had been in a deep coma and had been revived. Her voice was the sweetest sound in my life, and it never failed to resuscitate my weary being.

During the course of all those phone conversations, and through the stream of letters we exchanged back and forth, we learned almost everything about one another and ourselves. The love we felt was as pure and powerful as two lovers could ever imagine. We spoke about the future and about our personal lives, first separately and then together. Was it possible or even realistic to be traveling down this road when we hadn't yet been together physically very much—in fact, only a handful of times?

Our physical contact had been interrupted by an externally enforced absence, but through intense discussions and numerous letters that revealed every facet of our minds, our relationship flourished in an unprecedented way. Through our numerous dialogues, we were able to discover ourselves and one another in a depth unknown by any of our friends. This time of physical separation, which seemed horrible and interminable to us, emerged as an interval of amazingly deep emotional and intellectual enrichment.

We talked about music and books. Separately, during the daytime, we listened to and read the various pieces that had been brought up in our nocturnal discussions. The themes in contemporary music (especially folk music, in general, and Bob Dylan, in particular) fed the growing fire of our intellects. We both read and discussed J. D. Salinger's *Catcher in the Rye, Franny and Zooey, Raise High the Roof Beam Carpenters*, and *Seymour: An Introduction* and Steinbeck's *Travels with Charley in Search of America*. We were excited about reading and then discussing the ideas and themes we discovered in works of literature.

There were two works that significantly influenced my thinking at that critical time: Bob Dylan's song "Like a Rolling Stone" and J. D. Salinger's novel *Catcher in the Rye*. The sense of alienation that I have felt throughout my life was never more acute than when I was forcibly separated from my first love. No separation is worse than one between soul mates.

> *How does it feel*
> *To be on your own*
> *With no direction home*
> *Like a complete unknown*
> *Like a rolling stone?*
> From: "Like a Rolling Stone" by Bob Dylan

The sentiment of Dylan's song became imbedded in my being. The stark sense of reality in his song greatly appealed to me. The narrator, whom I strongly identified with, was able to see through the phoniness of people who tried to cast illusions about who they were and what they represented. Dylan was the voice of reason and clarity in a world filled with smoke and mirrors. He was the quintessential outsider, and I aspired to be such a voice. I wanted to face the realities of the world I lived in and to find the piercing truths behind the facade. Bob Dylan, reluctantly and involuntarily, became the most influential sage for most thinking people of my generation.

As for Holden Caulfield in *Catcher in the Rye*, his role of an outsider paralleled the force I felt within. His circumstances were different than mine, but the echo of his aloneness resonated within me. Marilyn and I both felt alone, but we were together. We were in separate geographic locations, but our emotional lives had been woven together into one intimate, dynamic fabric. The person I fell in love with evolved into the most important and influential person in my life, someone who permeated every part of my existence and my every thought.

Her daily letters reached me after summer school classes. The scent of her perfume on them made my heart race with anticipation to devour them. I was instantly transformed, and my everyday world without Marilyn became a distant second priority. The letters were tactile proof and confirmation that those all-night phone conversations were not just fantasies of a romantic young man. It reaffirmed the now-central axiom of my life: I lived for her and her alone. Everything I did throughout every single day was done to keep me occupied, to pass the time, until the magical ringing of an isolated telephone in the still of the night.

The Awakening and a Sacred Vow

When I think back to that chaotic night of June 4, 1965, I believe with all my heart that if anything worse had happened to Marilyn, I probably would have lost my mind—or worse. After those precious hours on the beach with the fire flickering in front of us, the waves gently breaking on the rocks, and the moon and stars emerging in the sky after the crimson sunset faded, I had fallen deeply in love with Marilyn. I would never be more certain about anything. That fact was, and would always remain, the single greatest truth of my life. And I knew it then, in those inaugural hours, as it was unfolding.

The reality I found myself in after the accident that night would've discouraged almost anyone. I was a high school dropout, not gainfully employed, and a child of a recently broken home without clear prospects for the future. I had certain abilities and an inexhaustible reservoir of optimism deep inside of me. I believed that much good awaited me in my life ahead. The turmoil and havoc facing me would be overcome. I could feel a positive surge of energy that seemed to contradict the events pummeling my youthful psyche at the time. I was just seventeen years old and pretty much on my own.

I had no one to whom I could turn for sound counsel and advice. I could not rally my life around the trite platitudes and simplistic offerings that others proffered with ease and little deliberation. "There are other fish in the sea" was a common piece of advice given to me with regard to dating other people. Some suggested I just walk away from Marilyn and my commitment to her. My disdain and distrust of easy clichés seriously crystallized during that period of time.

My mother gave me unconditional love and moral support. She was the single constant bright light emerging from the ruins of our shattered family. Her task of trying to keep our family together was daunting. The effort and energy this required was so all-encompassing that she needed to concentrate most of her focus and energy exclusively on the basics. She knew she could trust my judgment and completely believed in my abilities. But my mother needed to center her attention on keeping a roof over the family's head and becoming both mother and father for my younger brother and sister. Her personal loss of a husband was left out of her daily challenges. She would be alone without the man she had faithfully loved for twenty-two years. And never once did she complain about her private fate and secret loneliness.

Facing the upheaval and confusion, I turned inward to my own intellect for solace and self-guidance. Taking a *regular* job, and getting back on track in school with the goal of graduating with the class I had quit in the winter of 1965, was the beginning. My continued contact with Marilyn, in whatever form I could achieve it, became paramount. Writing letters and having inexhaustible telephone conversations with her were staples of my life as much as eating, sleeping, and breathing.

I took my goals on with a fierce sense of purpose and was resolved to succeed in them. The physical separation, although cruel and painful, fortified my desire to be with Marilyn. But, as I've said, the extensive telephone conversations would allow both of us to get to know each other in the most profound way. Although we were only seventeen years old, we had matured dramatically. Few people, never mind seventeen-year-olds, could have entered into such an intimate intellectual and emotional bond through pure dialogue. Always faced by the uncertainty of interruption in our nightly telephone conversations, we spoke deeply and honestly, and with a sense of heightened urgency, about all subjects. I counseled her, and she counseled me.

These discourses continued nightly, seven days a week, week after week into and through all of July and into August. Every day seemingly started with the We Five's song and moved through summer school classes, afternoons writing and reading love letters, and working at Super Duper to a focused motorcycle ride through the silent night to a clandestine telephone booth. There I excitedly awaited a ring that aroused my soul and set off a firework display in my heart. This schedule of intimate phone dialogue followed by school and work continued night after night, week after endless week. By the time August arrived, both she and I had reached the most glorious and inevitable truth of our young lives. Our love, although denied even the normal physicality most new lovers shared, had blossomed in a most remarkable and esoteric way.

During our conversation on Friday, August 13, 1965, having embraced the extraordinary scope and reality of our pure love, I boldly proposed my life and love to Marilyn, and she accepted with the same joy and commitment as I offered it to her. In the darkness of that night, two people holding telephones, separated by seven miles and a galaxy, wept tears of profound joy. The turmoil and pain in our young lives gave way to the most exquisite and intimate happiness a man and a woman could share together. We pledged our love *forever*. It was a vow, *our vow*. And it would seal our fate together for *eternity*.

To place this in context, one need only look at the pursuits of my friends and acquaintances. Their activity involved getting high (in those days by drinking), meeting girls with whom the primary purpose was to engage in casual sex, hanging out at a pool hall or coffee shop, and, generally, looking for temporal fun. It was perfectly normal behavior for adolescence and was rooted in the present moment with little or no reflection about personal growth or the future. Few spoke about college, ambition, or dreams and none about marriage.

My life had irrevocably changed. I was living a dream, my most cherished dream, and had great new dreams. My life had become defined and joyous in ways most of my friends couldn't even imagine. Over the next several months, our dreams would come into focus. Marilyn and I not only dreamt fantastic dreams but actually began planning them. We believed that all of our cherished dreams were achievable as long as we were together. We had one guiding, unshakable truth at the core of our lives: our love was total, complete, and as pure as any positive force either of us had ever experienced. No matter how awful life got, we both knew we had the other's love wholly, completely, and absolutely, and each of us was a refuge for the other. Nothing was impossible if we were together. It was a lover's Cartesian axiom: *I love and am loved; therefore, I am.* The certainty I felt in that relationship would never again grace my life.

Marilyn's letters, intoxicatingly scented with her perfume, reinforced our spoken words of love. Our nightly exchanges, although permeated with those words, were freeform discussions about everything from fashion to civil rights and folk music to Vietnam. Both of us were bright and well informed, and our discussions were constantly interesting. Our letters were narrowly focused on our mutual passion and love. At our tender age, although we were both literary leaning, written words flowed ever so slowly, so it was necessary to limit those concentrated written words to the most important part of our expanding relationship. That, of course, meant our words of love for one another.

Written words were frozen in time, whereas the spoken words were of the moment and alive in an essential way. The sound of our voices could be heard in the text of our love letters, but the live telephone conversations possessed a living, immediate vitality. We came to feel the significance and importance of our nightly conversations. They were the closest means we had to staying physically connected. It was abstract, but with a difference. Like sustenance, we needed to talk every night without fail—no matter what.

* * *

Chapter Five

Renewed Acquaintances and a Nautical Misadventure

My daily schedule, although rigid and full, allowed me to keep my sanity in some real sense. During the week, I went to summer school, had an afternoon break, worked at the supermarket in the evening, and then traveled to a prearranged rendezvous point to pick up a ringing telephone precisely at eleven p.m. Once the receiver touched my ear and I heard Marilyn's voice, I felt reborn.

There were times during the summer of 1965 when I found myself not in summer school and not working at Super Duper. Summer school classes ran mornings, Monday through Friday, and I usually worked on most of those days in the evening. But on occasion, I was free during the day on Saturday or Sunday afternoon. Generally, I would use my free time to write letters to Marilyn, reread her letters, or read books we had heard about from friends or each other. I spent minimal time studying for summer school, since I could recall almost everything my teachers said in class (a useful gift that made conventional studying unnecessary).

That year the most popular place to go was Bay Beach, which was located next to Crystal Beach Amusement Park in Canada. It was ten miles from the Peace Bridge that linked the United States to Canada. The usual recreational activities were swimming, playing beach football, or just strolling along the shoreline talking about life, observing people and the details of the homes of affluent people that jealously guarded access to the white, sandy shore. Walking along the pristine beach and clear water, talking with friends about aspects of our lives, was both entertaining and stimulating. The most sincere and genuine discussions I had with my friends happened as we casually strolled along the shores of the beach. Once we were in a relaxed atmosphere, away from personal landmarks, people would speak their minds, and we could connect in a meaningful way. This often worked when you were with one other person but almost never with three or more people. Some sort of devilish chemistry would occur, and the only goal would be laughter.

On one of those rare Saturdays that summer, the weather was clear, and I didn't need to be to work until five p.m. I drove up to Bay Beach by myself on my motorcycle, arriving at ten a.m. with the simple intention of spending some free time with any of my friends who might appear. I needed some sun and water time to help me break away from the school and work routine, to essentially disconnect from the intensity of my life. Water and sunshine were a sure prescription for giving my hyperactive mind some much-needed relief from thinking.

Once I settled in on my blanket, my friend Lenny I.'s cousin, Vinnie, arrived and set up his blanket next to mine. We spoke for a short time, and I listened to him attentively because he was more current on happenings involving our friends and acquaintances. Soon afterward, we were joined by another friend, Sean M., whose large family, it so happened, had a summer cottage just behind the beach where all of us were sitting. It was still early, and the beach was relatively empty. We had seen days like this and knew it was shaping up to be a later crowd, which meant our regular clique would be arriving between one and two p.m. Sean, Vinnie, and I found ourselves a little restless. Once we all expressed a certain common boredom and a little frustration over not being able to engage in a beach football game for many hours, if at all, Sean proposed an intriguing option.

His family's boat, a modest fourteen-foot aluminum craft with a compact outboard motor, was a few yards away by the fence that separated the rented summer cottages from the sandy beach where we were sitting. Sean offered to take our little group on a maritime excursion. Vinnie and I jumped at the suggestion, since no other recreational option was in sight.

We dragged the rather petite, lightweight craft across the white sand to the water's edge, launched it into the water until we were knee deep, and then hopped in. Vinnie and I watched Sean turn on the gas and pull a cord to start the engine. It started after a few tugs on the cord, making the modest sound of a glorified lawnmower. It belched small puffs of white smoke and, to our amazement, began to move our little boat. Sean worked the simple tiller and began to aim us perpendicularly away from shore. He asked Vinnie and me: "Where to?" Vinnie suggested Thunder Bay, which was about three or four nautical miles down the coast. Sean aimed his aluminum wonder in that general direction, and off we headed.

But a short time later, I suddenly got a brainstorm. "Why go to Thunder Bay just a few short miles down the shoreline? Why not do something bold and truly adventuresome?" I said.

"Like what?" both said at once. Without hesitation, I responded: "Let's go to Point Breeze!" They both readily agreed—never mind that we had no navigation system, an unknown quantity of gasoline, no life preservers, and no idea of how long it would take to make the round trip diagonally across the width of Lake Erie. These were mere details our young, adventuresome spirits could not be bothered with.

How far was it across Lake Erie to Point Breeze? How long would it take? How far would our fuel take us? What was the nautical forecast? We had absolutely no idea what the answers to these and other pertinent questions might be. However, we intuitively felt that we could make it there and back. The wind was calm, the water was as flat as an airport runway, and we took this as nature's personal invitation for us to make an impromptu trek.

Sean, at the helm of his concise little boat, opened it up for all it was worth. We skimmed effortlessly across the inviting blue calm like three intrepid explorers of some bygone era. Once we got far enough from the Canadian shoreline, we found ourselves puzzled by the fact that when we reached a certain distance from the shore we had left behind, we pretty much couldn't see either shore and became a little disoriented. We quickly decided to use the sun as a gauge to determine our direction.

Sean relinquished the tiller, first to Vinnie and then to me. All of us took turns navigating the route we had collectively mapped out orally. After a period of time (we had no watch, no drinking water, or any real gear other than a second small reserve gasoline tank), we could see what appeared to be the Boston Hills on the horizon. This set off a wave of optimism among our neophyte crew. Then, all of a sudden, out of nowhere it seemed, a speeding US Coast Guard boat overtook us.

They sternly inquired about where we came from and where we were going. After we timidly answered, they told us to put on our lifejackets. We had no lifejackets on board, so we cleverly took our square, foam-filled padded seats and began to attempt to poke our arms through the impossibly thin straps. We looked like we were complying, and, quickly and mysteriously, the Coast Guard boat roared off and vanished as rapidly as it had appeared. Sean and Vinnie looked at me, I looked at them, and we all began laughing. Boy, we fooled them; those dimwits thought we had a means of survival if our frail boat sank. *What idiots they are!* we all thought to ourselves. Our loud, hearty laughter bounced off the open water like well-thrown skipping stones before they sink to the bottom.

A few minutes later, we caught sight of the American shoreline and could actually see other boats and what appeared to be a marina. Sean retook the helm and guided us toward where we saw the greatest concentration of boats near the entrance to the marina. He expertly navigated up to a gas pump located on the outside of the marina, inquired about the price of their gasoline, and then turned to Vinnie and me to ante up. After filling both modest gas cans, we asked the pump attendant how far away was Point Breeze. Once he told us and we found out it was one thirty p.m., we decided to make our way back to Bay Beach. I had to get to work later in the afternoon, and we would have to go through our journey in reverse with new variables.

This time Vinnie took the tiller and began to navigate our course back across international waters toward Canada. Within a few minutes, the winds unexpectedly picked up, and our heretofore calm water began to get quite choppy. Our boat started bobbing up and down like an aquatic piston. We also felt the boat rocking left and then right, sliding side to side. Our bodies started absorbing a watery pounding. As the waves increased in size, Vinnie slowed our speed correspondingly. We began moving more and more slowly, and the prospect of reaching Bay Beach before Christmas was in serious jeopardy. The thought of having life preservers, which we had scoffed and laughed at, began to take hold of us.

I took the tiller from Vinnie and told him to prepare himself for what was certain to be a very bumpy ride. I asked him to take the seat (there were three in a row) closest to the bow and brace himself. Sean sat in the middle seat, and I sat by the motor near the stern with my right hand clutching the throttle. In the short time I had owned my motorcycle, I had earned a reputation as a bit of a daredevil, doing all sorts of tricks that required an uncanny sense of balance. Most of my friends regularly dumped their bikes, but it would be over five thousand kilometers of riding before I'd wipe out. This keen ability gave me a certain extra latitude when I took the tiller of our Lake Erie Kon-Tikki.

Vinnie was an athletic, wiry, 6'4" tall. Sean was several inches shorter than him, and I was a muscular 5'5" tall. Once I throttled-up and we achieved our top speed, we began to take quite a beating from the impact of our boat as it ricocheted off successive wave after wave. The bow of the boat was elevated because of the weight near the stern. Vinnie, who was tall and lanky, seemed like a giant in front of Sean and me. He had managed to wedge the silly-looking foam seat onto his back. He looked like Herman Munster, and his hands, tightly grasping either side of the cross board he was sitting on, held him in place like the support ropes of a circus tent. Sean and I openly laughed as we watched the boat violently bouncing up and down and from side to side with Vinnie sitting perfectly stationary in front of us.

Luck was on our side. As we recklessly plowed through the rough waves, we reached a point where the winds shifted direction. The water miraculously flattened out, and we were spared any further pounding. As if by magic, we were again gliding through smooth water with the Canadian shoreline coming into sight. I felt a sense of relief knowing that not only would we make it back to Bay Beach but I would also be able to get back to Buffalo and to my job at Super Duper on time.

Before I relinquished the controls back to Sean, I decided one more prank would be in order to complete the day's memorable festivities. We were speeding along at full throttle when, a couple miles from shore, I turned off the gas. Our boat went dead in the water. Sean knew what I had done; Vinnie didn't. I then told Vinnie, "Our luck ran out. We'll have to swim to shore."

Vinnie accepted my grim assessment without question. He stood up and began twisting and contorting his body to adjust the impossibly small, useless seat cushion attached to his back. The sight of him standing in front of us, like a giant readying himself for the long, impossible swim to shore, was just too much. Sean and I burst out laughing before Vinnie actually took a plunge into the water. As I was laughing, I blurted out, "Sit back down." Vinnie, somewhat embarrassed by this practical joke, took his seat. Sean took the tiller and with great skill opened up the engine and raced back to the shore where we had started our foolhardy odyssey. All of us were quite sunburned, tired, and hungry, but we had a great story about a youthful adventure we would never repeat.

After we reached shore and dragged our surprisingly hardy craft back to its original resting place, I said good-bye and walked back to my motorcycle. Although I was burnt beet red, famished, and exhausted, I felt great relief that for a little time my mind and body had been far removed from my normal routine. I mounted my little Yamaha, happy to have escaped the city for six hours, and drove back home to get ready for my shift at Super Duper and, more importantly, a phone conversation with my beloved in the wee hours of the morning.

Her Voice: Sustenance for My Soul

When Marilyn spoke to me, her words traveled through my ear into my brain, and life flowed through my veins. I was obsessively driven to get to whatever phone booth we had chosen for our nightly conversation. As I said, eleven p.m. was picked for two reasons: her parents would be sound asleep, and I would be done with work at Super Duper. The latter occurred between ten and ten fifteen p.m. like clockwork—usually.

But on one occasion, this schedule was in grave jeopardy because an assistant manager decided to extend the workload on our shift. Once the store closed at nine p.m., we had to restock as many of the shelves in the store as we could, incinerate all the empty cardboard boxes and trash, sweep all the aisles, and then, finally, mop all the floor areas where customers walked. Almost every night was identical to the previous one, and within ninety minutes, at the very most, we were done.

One night, a newer manager, Dick D., decided to flex his managerial muscles by expanding our tasks in such a way as to add time to our shift. He obviously wanted to demonstrate to his bosses and the corporate element that he was superior to his managerial counterparts by getting more work out of his tired underlings. Unfortunately for him, he wasn't aware of my higher priority: namely, being at a predetermined phone booth at the stroke of eleven p.m.

It was quite clear to me that if we did everything our taskmaster was asking us to do, we would be working until at least eleven p.m. or later still, which was well past our usual quitting time. My coworkers and I worked hard and long, and to arbitrarily extend our night shift seemed cruel and capricious to me. The thought of not being in position to answer my telephone call from Marilyn at the stroke of eleven, caused a surge of adrenalin to race through my body.

No one worked in the incinerator room as vigorously as I. I'd collect empty cardboard boxes from the stock boys working in their particular aisles, break them down, and then shove them into the blazing incinerator. Once I opened the steel door, the intense heat would escape into the small, enclosed area, which had all cinder block walls. I had to continually rake over the fire with a long steel pole that had a hoe-like end piece. This allowed some of the molten ashes to drop through a grate that, when cooled, could be removed from outside the back of the building. It was not uncommon for the hoe end and part of the steel shaft of the pole to get red hot, which necessitated wearing asbestos gloves to protect your hands when you held it. I often worked shirtless in that infernally concise space.

After raking the ashes, I would shove in more trash until the incinerator was full again and then close the heavy, thick steel door by its metal chain and pulleys. The hot seven-foot pole was placed standing against a cinder block wall with the hoe end on the concrete floor. I learned early in my career as an *incinerator man* how important it was to carefully choose a spot for that tool.

Once, while I was getting my next load ready for the incinerator, I took a false step backward and stepped on the hoe end, causing the hot pole to fall onto my shirtless back like a branding iron. Thank goodness I had catlike reflexes and quickly lunged away as the hot metal started to touch my naked back. The burn was superficial enough for a complete, scarless recovery, but the experience gave me a healthy awareness of where I placed my dangerously hot tool in the future.

The night of Dick D.'s attempt to extend our shift, I became alarmed by the prospect of the ringing of an unanswered public phone. I moved as fast as a jaguar to expedite the chores on our extended list. I collected debris on a four-wheel cart and ran back and forth to my incinerator room. I loaded and transported cases of stock out to the corresponding aisles to keep my fellow workers supplied with the stock for their shelves. I worked like two men, but it became clear that we wouldn't be leaving in time for me to get to my designated telephone booth by eleven p.m. I felt a certain growing panic building within me.

Something needed to be done to abbreviate this work shift, something fast. Divine intervention was immediately ruled out, and a wave of nihilism came over me. I had the unilateral answer to this dilemma that would be the solution not only for this night but for any night that an overzealous manager wanted to make a statement.

It was half past ten, and my coworkers were finishing stocking shelves. In a few minutes, we would all be called on to sweep the floors of the entire store and then mop every aisle and public area. Before the final phase was to begin, I disappeared into the backroom, collected every broom and every mop (six or eight of each), and rushed into the incinerator room. I opened the steel door and rapidly fed all the mops and brooms into the red-hot embers. Each tool spontaneously burst into flames and, within only a few minutes, was reduced to homogeneous material, leaving behind no incriminating trace.

Dick, seeing the shelves replenished, waved his small, clawlike hand to his weary minions to begin sweeping and preparing for mopping the store. Several of us began filling the special oversized pails with soapy water, readying them for the final stage of the job after the sweeping was completed. But within a couple of minutes, everyone stopped everything they were doing to join in a semidesperate search for what appeared to be missing brooms and mops.

Dick went outside the building to see if someone had uncleverly tossed the missing tools into the parking lot or threw them into the large Dumpster. No sign could be found anywhere inside the store or outside the building. It was as perplexing as an alien abduction, one of those great mysteries that would be talked about for a long time. With no other choice, we were released from our bondage.

Within minutes, I would be lifting a telephone receiver and hearing the voice that would again thaw my soul and breathe new life into my world. The mystery of the missing brooms and mops would remain so into the next century, when it'd be revealed in the pages of a love story.

Pilgrimage to a Forbidden Place

Our ritual and routine of letters and phone calls continued through June, all of July, and into August, as I mentioned. After we had pledged our love and life on August 13, we both grew impatient with the cruelty of our separation. We decided to tempt fate by getting together.

Marilyn had a cast on her left leg below her knee and was unable to go anywhere without the greatest effort and the use of crutches. Before she became ambulatory with a walking cast, we agreed to meet on her porch after her parents retired and spend whatever time we could in an in-person, live conversation, the first real one since the last time we were together in her hospital room back in early June. A night was picked for our secret reunion.

> *When I'm feelin' blue, all I have to do,*
> *Is take a look at you, then I'm not so blue ...*
> *When you're close to me, I can feel your heartbeat,*
> *I can hear you breathing in my ear ...*
> From: "A Groovy Kind of Love" by The Mindbenders

I drove through the night retracing my route for our first date back in June. During my ride to her house, I wished this was my first time driving the route back before the accident. I wished I could've been transported back in time with the knowledge I now possessed. I visualized a different route and a different outcome. Marilyn could've been spared her pain and suffering, and we could've shared the long, beautiful summer (which was soon coming to an end) together.

I carefully parked my white Yamaha a couple of blocks away from her house and proceeded on foot in the darkness like some sort of Green Beret commando toward where she lived. My heart was beating fiercely as if trying to escape my chest. Once I approached her home, I saw her physical outline propped up on a glider couch on their narrow, first-floor South Buffalo porch, which faced south. As I got closer and closer, her faint image filled into a living, flesh and blood, real-life form. Her entire face seemed to have an angelic halo around it. Her hair was long and blonde, her eyes as enchantingly blue as the waters of Barbados, her skin flawlessly smooth and perfect.

Our eyes locked onto one another's, and, as I approached the last few feet, our extended arms and hands touched and entwined. We pulled close together until our lips met in a short but deeply passionate kiss. I uttered in a hushed, emotional whisper, "I love you with all my heart!"

Then she echoed my mantra: "I love you, my darling, with all my heart too!" I could smell her perfume, Wind Song by Prince Machiabelli, and it enveloped me in its glorious scent. We embraced tightly, and her warm, silky, magnificent skin and hair touched my face. Nothing and no one else in the world mattered: I had stepped into Eden and was with my Eve.

We spoke in serious, impassioned whispers, holding hands tightly and embracing repeatedly. It had been many long, lonely days and weeks of yearning for this very moment. Neither of us took it for granted. It was like a holy pilgrimage to a sacred site, and we believed that what was happening was nothing less than a miracle. Our spoken words were a summary of our many written love letters. Her live, in-person voice was music for my heart. The sensation of her warm, smooth, fragrant, living flesh against mine sent me into a kind of religious ecstasy.

On her cramped porch, we continued to speak softly, lovingly, and hurriedly, knowing that our precious reunion could come to an unwanted, abrupt end. Marilyn's parents told her it was due to the lawsuit that we must be apart and have no contact. The fact that I was not a South Buffalo Irish American also played a role in our being kept from seeing one another. Both Marilyn and I believed in equality of all people. We measured people by their individual qualities, not ethnic background, gender, or any of those other false measuring sticks of human worth.

I had yet to meet Marilyn's two younger brothers, Harry and Jimmy. Their loyalty was still in question, so we had to be wary of four people. After a short time by our telephone conversation standard, we heard an unknown noise from within the house. In an instant, I leaped over the porch railing and sliced through the bush that divided her house from Kathy M.'s house. Off I ran, like a phantom in the night, at a speed which would have won a winner's patch back when I was on my high school track team.

Soon I found myself on my trusty Yamaha heading toward the West Side. The scent of her perfume was embedded in my shirt, the sound of her sweet, live, in-person voice echoed in my ears, the sensation of her warm kiss tingled on my lips, and the image of the two of us together danced in my deliriously happy head. It was *true*, she was *real*, our love was *great*, and our life together would be *beautiful*. Happiness had now adorned our world, and future possibilities suddenly felt boundless.

> *Your arms and hands … and mine*
> *Entwine*
> *Your lips and smile … and mine*
> *Combine*
> *Your heart and body … and mine*
> *Touch*
> *Your joy and happiness … and mine*
> *Connect*
> *Your dreams and hopes … and mine*
> *Merge*
> *Your mind and soul … and mine*
> *Converge*
> *Your present and future … and mine*
> *Together.*

A Vision in Daylight

As fantastic as our reuniting had been, the danger and potential consequences of being caught together on her porch would outweigh a repeat performance. We were in treacherous water, and any miscalculation could result in even greater sanctions. Our young, eager spirits were overruled by good judgment. We knew we would eventually be together; the future was ours, but the present time must be dealt with caution and delicacy. Our insatiable need to be together as much as possible would be fulfilled in the near future. But for the short term, so it seemed, our love letters and nighttime telephone conversations would have to suffice. We had no choice but to control the passionate fire burning within us.

The lesson of that splendid night was that we could not repeat being together at ground zero: her house. Shortly after our physical reunion, Marilyn was fitted with a walking cast, which gave her a modest degree of mobility. Again, our imaginative minds concocted a new, more viable plan to be together—and this time in broad daylight.

Knowing how avid a reader Marilyn was, her mother readily gave her permission to take a taxicab to the local branch library less than a mile away from home. The modest library was on the edge of Cazenovia Park, an old, beautiful, historic Olmsted park. We would meet there in broad daylight and talk in person and embrace and kiss when the opportunity afforded itself.

Every time I was with her, the boundary of my love was extended. The power of the growing love I had for her was the first suggestion I would have of certainty and truth. My whole world increasingly became predicated upon cultivating and protecting our relationship. The more my love for Marilyn expanded, the more the rest of the world became less important. All my other activities would be done to whatever degree necessary to help facilitate that relationship and every moment we spent together.

> Cher: *They say we're young and we don't know*
> *We won't find out until we grow*
>
> Sonny: *Well I don't know if all that's true*
> *'Cause you got me, and I got you.*
> From: "I Got You Babe" by Sonny & Cher

During our meetings at the branch library, we'd leave the building and go off into the picturesque park. We talked, we held hands, and we embraced whenever we had the privacy to do so. But mostly, we basked in the powerful synergy of our expanding, fearless love. The certainty we felt about our love for one another was true. Over forty years later, light years from my youth, I have come to realize that my love for Marilyn was the only great truth I would experience in my life. Although my life would be filled with many amazing events and other loves, my love for Marilyn would remain alive, vibrant, and everlasting beneath the layers of life I have lived. I recognized the scope, impact, and power of my love for her from our first time together alone on the beach on our first date. Our love was *"a love that was more than love."* We both recognized it from the very start.

* * *

CHAPTER SIX

≡

A Wall Is Taken Down/ A Foreign World Is Revealed

A few weeks after our secret meetings at the library, an unforeseen event occurred. To this day I have never learned the exact reason for her parents' change of heart.

Mrs. S., along with her husband, unexpectedly announced to Marilyn that the wall of our separation was taken down and I would be welcomed into their home. Perhaps my gainful employment and academic reinstatement caused them to reassess my worthiness to see their only daughter. Since the night of the accident, much in my life had changed, not to mention my appearance. My beard was shaved off, and my hair, too, was cropped and *respectable.*

For me, my beard and longish hair were just outward manifestations of my objection to the phony, superficial world around me. Internally, intellectually, my rebellious spirit remained unscathed and alive. But the outside world, which places far too much stock on outward appearances, perceived a conventional late-teen youth. They couldn't have been more incorrect in their appraisal of who I was or what I was thinking. This facade proved a convenient cover for who I really was and what I would do in my life.

Often, I was invited to dinner with Marilyn's family. Their home was immaculately clean, and everything was neatly in its place. Although they had a dog named Bucky (a black and white cocker spaniel), one could not detect any scent or sign of his presence. The living room furniture consisted of an area rug, a six-foot-long couch near the entranceway, several chairs, end tables, and a coffee table positioned toward the television set on the far wall. Every floor was vacuumed and every surface dusted. The typical living room led to the dining area that was connected to the kitchen. There were four bedrooms on the second floor, an area I would never see. It all was simple and complete, and it reflected a wholeness of their family unit. Mrs. S. kept the house in perfect order. She even did laundry daily to keep everyone's wardrobes continuously replenished.

Marilyn's father was the central figure at the dinner table; he spoke first and commented on all statements made by Marilyn, Harry, Jimmy, or Mrs. S. Marilyn's mother lived the life of a dedicated wife and mother of a bygone era. She capitulated to her husband's every wish and command. He, on the other hand, was often short and abrupt with her. You could easily see how he assumed superiority and authority over her and his descendants.

His somewhat laconic opinions were derived from his personal observations and interactions in the real world. Personally, I never saw him reading books or heard him mention books he had read. He read the newspaper daily, watched television news, and generated gut feelings and observations about the increasingly confusing world of the mid-1960s. In 1965, he was a hardworking man in his early seventies. At that time, civil rights had taken center stage, the Vietnam *conflict* was escalating, and young people of his daughter's generation were beginning to demand answers about those issues. Civil order seemed to be under assault.

Mr. S. was a man who became an engineer on the Norfolk & Western Railroad and had risen up through the ranks. Whatever task was asked of him he completed. His world, in that long-ago place, involved a loyalty to the employer that is all but nonexistent in the twenty-first century. In those days, when you took a job, you probably were taking a job for life. The employer often superseded your family in some sense. You did everything you were asked to do without complaint. Often, no union existed to intervene on behalf of an overworked or mistreated worker. Too often the unions that did exist became aligned with their corporate counterparts, and the benefit of being a card-carrying union member was impossible to discern. In that environment, you were either a union man or a company man. Mr. S. had lived through the evolution and conflicts between management and unions and had become toughened, hardened, and, perhaps, too pragmatic.

He was a man truly fixed in his thinking. He knew what he knew; there was little room for actual discussion or debate. Perhaps that's the reason change and situations outside the everyday flow of common activities raised his ire. It required thought and consideration and the chance for mistakes in judgment. Common sense regarding common things worked most of the time in everyday life, but once more complicated issues arose, common sense was simply not good enough.

I certainly qualified as a *variable* in Mr. S.'s fixed universe. I drove a motorcycle, came from a broken home, had been a temporary high school dropout, and, worse yet, seemed independent. Although I was respectful and polite, I did not capitulate to his dominant will. And I made it known early on that my love for their daughter was sincere and I would do *anything* for her. No one could change my feelings for her. Her father, perhaps sensing my commitment and dedication to her, allowed me into his home and their world. Although I took my place alongside Marilyn, I never saw myself in that world indefinitely and instead felt a new sense of purpose and a need to make more defined plans for my future with Marilyn.

Back in June, which was the time of high school examinations and graduation, Marilyn had been unable to participate in either. College had been discussed; after all, she was a bright honor student and a young woman with a keen intellect. But an academic hiatus occurred after the accident. Given that she wasn't making immediate plans to attend college, and that her injured leg was still on the mend, she applied for a job in downtown Buffalo in the fall of 1965. It was a clerical, entry-level job that paid the standard minimum wage of the time (one dollar per hour).

Focused Goals and a Renewed Purpose

During the early part of autumn, I continued working at Super Duper, usually twenty-five to thirty hours per week, while I attended high school full time with my original fellow senior classmates. The Friday night graveyard shift eventually became a regular part of my schedule at work. I'd arrive at eleven p.m. and join in the cleaning of the store by sweeping the aisles, mopping floors, restocking shelves, and organizing the stockroom for the morning shipment. Saturday was the busiest day of the week at Super Duper, and every effort was needed to accommodate and prepare for it.

As the restocking of the shelves was being done, I would collect the empty cardboard boxes and burnable debris and dispose of them in our incinerator. The heat generated by that furnace would prepare me for my future years working in the relentless heat at the archaic steel mill in Lackawanna. I developed an impressive tolerance for temperatures over a hundred degrees.

After we worked all night preparing the store for its Saturday rush, at around six a.m. our delivery truck would arrive with between one and two thousand cases of food items, which needed to be unloaded from the truck and coherently stacked in the stockroom. Prior to unloading the truck, a metal conveyor belt with steel rollers needed to be assembled like a giant Lionel train set. Once it was in place, the truck driver would start manually sliding case after case of various food items into the building.

With the help of one other worker, most often my friend Tom D., I would remove the cases off the conveyor belt and stack them on wooden pallets along the walls of the storeroom. One of us would lift cases (which could weigh as much as forty pounds) off the conveyor and literally toss them through the air to the other person, who would carefully catch and stack the cases by item, usually floor to ceiling. The key to segregating the cases was to have the labels on the boxes facing outward and to group them logically. For instance, we once received a shipment of four hundred cases of soft drink (twenty-four twelve-ounce cans per case), which were stacked by flavor.

Tom and I were like a machine, seldom falling behind the continuous stream of cases sliding down the conveyor belt. In fact, we were so good at it that the Saturday shipment (the largest and most important one of the week) became our exclusive assignment. Managers usually would oversee the work of their underlings and flex their authority by offering constant or unsolicited suggestions for improvement. Tom and I were left alone, largely because we were so efficient and never complained about the work being too hard or too physical. We thrived on the challenge of the physical labor of the job and actually had fun doing it. We were a different breed.

At the conclusion of our shift at about eight a.m., I would go home to Fargo Avenue, clean up, and head off to Marilyn's house on G. Street or meet her in downtown Buffalo, whichever got us together quicker. When the weather turned too cool or rainy, we would take buses from our respective homes to a meeting place in downtown Buffalo. For a number of weeks into the fall, when the weather was good enough, I would drive my motorcycle to South Buffalo, park a couple of blocks away from G. Street, and then walk to Marilyn's house. Her parents assumed that we would be taking public buses, and we said nothing to crush their illusion.

Marilyn had no problem getting back on my motorcycle. She trusted me completely and knew I would never do anything to jeopardize our well-being. Like me, she knew we probably were alive because we had been on a motorcycle rather than in a car on June 4. Her faith in my abilities was only rivaled by my mother's. She empowered me with the courage to face any challenge and to feel fulfilled in ways I would never feel again.

Once we arrived in downtown Buffalo, the busy shopping center of Western New York, we would methodically walk from store to store, looking at outfits she'd model for me. She would solicit my opinion about each outfit: the color, the pattern, the hemline, the fabric. Believe me, this was no passive process; I had to give detailed reasons why I liked certain outfits more than others. I tried to be as honest and frank as I could possibly be. But the truth be known, she looked great to me no matter what she wore. Every second of every day with her was the fulfillment of a dream for me.

Store to store, outfit to outfit, we worked our way through the hectic, crowded downtown area. Hens and Kelley's, L.L. Berger's, David's, AM&A's, Hengerers': we marched through all the stores to every ladies' department. We walked upstairs, took escalators, or rode elevators. Along the way, we grabbed a quick bite to eat. Our Saturday routine was so regular that we were known by clerks in all the stores.

On one occasion, as I waited for Marilyn to emerge from a dressing room modeling an outfit that had caught her eye, a woman clerk came over to me to offer her condolences. She had observed our detailed discussions on several occasions and thought I must be distressed. Of course, the clerk had no idea how Marilyn and I had to suffer through the past summer. For me, being with Marilyn doing anything was a sublime pleasure. I told the clerk something to the effect of, "My love for her is so great, any activity with her is a pure joy." It was not the typical response from a young man waiting for his girlfriend in a women's clothing store. But then again, we were not a typical couple.

At the end of the Saturday shopping pilgrimage, we generally went back to her parents' house, where we would have dinner and watch television in their cozy living room. One by one, her family members retreated to their bedrooms upstairs. When we found ourselves alone, we would hug, embrace, and kiss. Our time alone was limited, so when we were able to be truly alone, we would take advantage of the opportunity to express our physical passion. Real intimacy would be ours in the near future, so we bided our time. We had learned tremendous patience during our long, arduous separation over the summer.

My departure from Marilyn's house was coordinated with the last Seneca Street bus to downtown Buffalo. (It left the city line at 11:06 p.m., not that I remember.) Once I arrived on Main Street in downtown, I walked a short distance to Shelton Square, a local bus terminal and historic landmark that would be torn down the next year in the name of progress. I would then catch the last outbound Niagara Street bus home.

But on occasion, Marilyn and I would fall asleep in each other's arms on the couch and I would miss the last Seneca Street bus to downtown Buffalo. Remember: I went to school on Friday morning, worked all night at Super Duper until Saturday morning, and then was with Marilyn all day until eleven p.m. I was up some forty-plus hours, attended a full day at school, worked eight or nine hours at the supermarket, shopped and walked downtown from midmorning until late afternoon, and then spent five hours at Marilyn's house. Missing the last bus meant I'd have to call a taxicab in order to make it home.

On Sunday mornings I would report to Super Duper at seven a.m. for the Sunday ritual of replenishing all the shelves, cleaning all the floors, and disposing of all the cardboard and burnable trash from the previous day's bustling activity. Saturdays were the busiest day of the week, and on Sundays the store was closed by law, the infamous blue law. It was a somewhat relaxed time, casual clothes were acceptable, and one got to work four or five hours.

Afterward, Marilyn and I would meet and spend the remainder of the day together, sometimes going to a movie in the afternoon or else either going to my mother's apartment or to Marilyn's house. Generally, we preferred Marilyn's house at the end of the day because it was easier for her to be at home when we said good night. My mother's apartment was much smaller, and there were just too many people to deal with. Harry and Jimmy, Marilyn's brothers, were younger than us, and both were easier to get along with than my siblings.

Humble Symbol of Eternal Love

By October 1965, I had saved about five weeks of gross earnings and bought a diamond engagement ring at Tanke's Jewelers on Main Street in downtown Buffalo. It was a modest but beautiful ring that symbolized the sincerity of my love for Marilyn. I gave it to her with great pride and love. It represented my devotion, my commitment, and my humble background. It was the first ring I had ever given anyone, and it formally and visually ended my boyhood and her girlhood. We symbolically left childhood and became a man and a woman.

Both of us felt a special pride as we gazed upon the radiant sparkle of that diminutive diamond ring. It became a rallying point for our spirits. As we looked at it, we saw many things. For Marilyn, it was the symbol of love from a struggling young man who would pass every test of love for her. For me, it represented the beginning of a relationship with the one person I would love forever. It was the seed we planted together that would blossom in *our* Garden of Eden, and it was to be the first of many flowers in that paradise.

During the fall of 1965, it became clear to me there was a serious clash between Marilyn and her father. Some of the discussions at the dinner table escalated into harsh arguments. A battle of wills unfolded before me, and Marilyn's beliefs and ideals were often under attack by someone incapable of opening his eyes to a different point of view. I found myself awkwardly in the middle as an observer. Poor Marilyn argued with her ancient father, who had graduated from high school before World War I, over a half century ago, in a world now buried in the dusty pages of an out-of-print book.

As so often with this type of argument, personal attacks were levied. They accomplished their odious goal: Marilyn was often distraught and hurt. Her father knew how to emotionally unhinge her, and he often did. As time passed, Marilyn and I knew she could not remain in that environment too much longer. I didn't know if her father wanted me to think less of her based on these demonstrations of his power to upset her in front of me. I did not think less of her; quite the contrary.

We spent every possible minute together around our jobs and my school schedule and never missed an opportunity to be together. Our love and dedication were apparent to the world. We held hands everywhere we went, and even a poor-sighted, one-eyed person could have seen that the love we emanated was no superficial teenage love. Every day our love seemed to grow. We talked about the details of our pasts, the present, and what was ahead in our life together. The future was ours; soon the adults who affected us negatively would be behind us, unable to influence or compromise our choices and dreams.

Before things reached a critical point, we were able to spend important quality time with our two families to really see one another's respective world up close and personally. My mother was now a single parent trying to keep our family together with little or no help from my wayward father, who had all but abandoned his first family. She trusted my judgment and allowed me more personal freedom than any of my friends had. My mother knew I was in love with Marilyn and was serious about our relationship. I believe Marilyn found relief in my mother's compassionate, loving approach. It was clear that my mother respected my opinions and work ethic. In contrast, Marilyn's father saw a woman's role to be a support system for the all-important male breadwinner of the family.

Marilyn heard about my parents' troubles and knew about my father's infidelity. I had been in her home, her world, and gotten to see the interactions of her family. Being there and talking with every member of her family gave me the opportunity to know what her life had been like before we met and to be acquainted with the most important players in it.

She had seen my family life on Fargo Avenue and was able to

see the circumstances of my life. We each were able to get a deeper understanding of the other as a result. We wanted to know as much about each other as possible because we knew this knowledge would allow our love to flourish and grow. But Marilyn's view of my family world was missing one crucial and critical piece of the puzzle: my father. Although I deplored what my father had done to our family and the way he had deeply hurt my mother, I still had love for him. I wanted to maintain a relationship with him even amid all the troubling and painful circumstances. That was yet another paradox to deal with.

One night I took Marilyn to meet my father at his place of employment: the Char-Pit Grill. I hoped we could share a few minutes of conversation and reveal our cherished plan for the future with him. When we arrived, the bar was not crowded, and it appeared the conversation about our expanding relationship could take place without too many interruptions.

* * *

CHAPTER SEVEN

‡

Meeting the Last Familial
Piece of the Puzzle

When you entered the bar from busy West Ferry Street, you found yourself in a space about twenty-five feet by about thirty-five feet. One section along the rear left area contained a partially walled-off open area housing the cooking pit (a *char-pit*) with overhead storage above and a compact three-foot refrigerator underneath. Between the entranceway and the cooking area were several wooden tables, surrounded by three to four wooden chairs apiece, and a jukebox loaded with a disproportionate number of Frank Sinatra tunes. To the right was a long, well-worn wooden bar extending nearly the length of the room. Behind it, on the wall, were shelves filled with various liquors. Below those shelves were short barroom refrigerators jammed with numerous brands of cooling bottled beers. Under the long wooden bar were beer taps connected to kegs of beer in the basement, a stainless steel sink and drain board for cleaning beer glasses, and sundry equipment to accommodate the bartender along his carpeted bartender-run between the back wall and bar.

Nearly everyone in the place smoked cigarettes or cigars, and years of this activity in this unventilated, confined space had saturated the pores of the walls and ceiling with immeasurable exhaled second-hand smoke from countless brands of tobacco products. A rusty yellow hue, only visible in daylight, covered every surface. The floor had been the beneficiary of many accidental spills of every brand of beer and liquor known to man and had retained a discernible stench, even after countless daily washings, that unmistakably announced what type of establishment you had entered. A smaller back room, with a half dozen wooden tables and chairs, was on the other side of a dividing wall beyond the char-pit cooking area. This was the center of my father's universe.

At the end of the bar, standing with a burning cigarette between her fingers, my father's mistress stood like a relaxed sentry casually watching the random activity in the bar. She had jet black hair, wore heavy makeup, and was more attractive than most of the plain, blue-collar women who frequented this gin mill. I had not anticipated Nina being there, but no matter. When my father was free from his bartending duties, I proudly introduced Marilyn to Nina and him. They asked perfunctory questions about her background and half-listened to her responses. Clearly, this was not important to either my father or his mistress. They were trying to be polite as best they could.

"Where do you live?" Nina asked as she continued to take deep puffs on her cigarette and turn her eyes away to watch the movements of the other people in the intimate space. After Marilyn politely responded, Nina then asked, "What school do you go to?" Again, her eyes scanned everything in the room but the person she was addressing. After each lame question, asked with not an inkling of interest, Nina would blandly say, "That's nice."

After Marilyn's brief interview, I jumped into the conversation to get to the heart of the reason why we were there. I proudly announced: "We're deeply in love, and we'll be getting married once I turn eighteen. We plan to go to California, where I'll attend college."

Instead of offering congratulations and words of support and encouragement, they both sarcastically snickered. Then both spoke patronizing words that were so obviously false, both Marilyn and I felt as if we had been slapped in the face. "Oh yeah, okay. Well, good luck with that. Sounds interesting," said my father, devoid of any sincerity whatsoever.

Nina repeated her hollow response, "That's nice," this time speaking through a partially repressed sneer. The visit and conversation was finished.

We left the Char-Pit and began to discuss what just had happened. Both Marilyn and I were deeply offended by the contempt we had just been shown. My father and his mistress had insulted our most cherished dream. Marilyn would never see my father again, and I would stop speaking with or seeing him for five years.

During September and October we were able to get a close glimpse into both of our worlds. The time we spent with one another's families allowed us to understand some of what we had spoken about during our countless hours of telephone conversations over the summer. The accuracy of our descriptions was revealed and confirmed by our numerous live visits to our respective homes. I found Marilyn's two younger brothers, Harry and Jimmy, to be two really nice young men who were very different from one another and very pleasant. They felt like real allies, and they were.

A First Step toward Independence

As I've said, Marilyn's father could be quite contentious at times, and his obvious effect upon her troubled me. Outside of the apparent and usual consequences of a splintered family, my mother's home was rather benign but lacked a sense of wholeness. As we moved deeper into fall, our first major family holiday, Thanksgiving, was on the horizon. We had to make a decision, as a couple, about how we would spend the holiday.

Before we met, each of us had spent all our holidays exclusively with our own family. The prospect of somehow splitting time between our two families was logistically impractical since my motorcycle was pretty much stored for the winter. The thought of being with both sides on the same day, even if we had a car, was not palatable in any way.

We found ourselves wanting to be alone together as much as possible. We had been forced to endure a terrible, unjust penance over the long summer, and we continually sought to be together by ourselves, unencumbered by family complications. She was the most articulate, fascinating, and beautiful woman I had ever known. When we were together, by ourselves, we were able to have rich conversations about an endless array of subjects and to feel the power and wonder of our magnificent, ever-growing love.

Marilyn and I chose to do something independent and memorable. We decided to have dinner together, just her and me, at a special place.

We made a reservation to dine at the newly opened, and rather exotic, Skylon Tower in Niagara Falls, Ontario. It was a restaurant like no other of the era. It had a revolving dining room at the top of a five-hundred-foot structure overlooking Niagara Falls. It rotated once an hour, and it was said you could see the skylines of Buffalo, Rochester, and Toronto on a clear night.

Since we didn't have a car, we had to rely on public transportation and Greyhound buses to get us there and back. We also would be required to get dressed up. I wore a brand new sport coat, slacks, and a shirt and tie bought for the occasion. Marilyn, who loved sewing, launched into making her own unique outfit. I accompanied her to a sewing store in downtown Buffalo to pick out a pattern and the material for her outfit. She ended up making a two-piece suit: a jacket and a skirt with rich green wool material from the pattern purchased at the store.

We had settled on the color green as *our* color because it symbolized the prime color of spring, which was the rebirth of life after winter. Both of us were an integral part of the rebirth of our two lives. We chose every facet of our collective life together with thoughtful care and passionate love. The actual holiday was exactly like any other typical day we spent together. My heart raced wildly upon seeing her. Then catching the mesmerizing scent of her fragrant perfume (usually Windsong), all my other senses were electrified. My eyes never grew weary of looking at her, and my heart could never hold more love for anyone. She was, and would always be, the only person I'd ever love so purely and so completely.

Our families, after hearing our independent plans, essentially made no protest since our arrangement favored neither side. The very day was almost dreamlike. Marilyn, in her handmade green wool suit, looked as beautiful and stunning as Jean Shrimpton or any other enchanting model that she had introduced me to in her many fashion magazines. The fact we would be taking buses to get to our first great dinner date was irrelevant to us. Just being together, dressed up in our new outfits under our similar beige London Fog trench coats, sitting close together, holding hands and feeling our bodies pressing against one another, made the day feel extraordinarily special. The diamond ring I had given her a month earlier adorned her hand and was a visible reminder that our love was special and sacred. The sparkle emitted from that humble diamond cast a glow over our two beings. How the outside world perceived it, and us, made no difference. The happiness we felt together was truly beyond words.

The bus we took from the old Greyhound bus terminal in downtown Buffalo left us about a mile and a half short of our final destination, so we walked the rest of the way filled with great expectation and joy. The weather that day was gray and dreary, but when your hearts are filled to capacity with love as ours were, all things are rendered not only tolerant and bearable but also wondrous.

As we headed toward the Skylon, we could barely see the imposing, towering structure through an unusual fog that had formed. Once we approached the parking lot, we saw a couple of external elevators that looked like yellow pods with clear glass doors sliding up and down the long neck of the Skylon Tower. At times, the structure below the summit that houses the restaurant and observation deck would vanish in the fog. Since the top of the Skylon is lit up with lights, it almost looked like an extraterrestrial craft hovering in space when the supporting shaft was cloaked in fog.

I was personally amazed by my effortless courage in stepping into a glass-door external elevator and going up some five hundred feet in space. Ten months earlier, before Plager and Stevenson, I would've fainted at the mere thought of riding such an elevator. But on that Thanksgiving Day, I was riding up into the clouds with a real-life angel. No biblical heaven could have elicited greater joy in my heart.

We marveled at the unusual structure, which looks similar to the Seattle Space Needle. Once we stepped off the elevator and entered the dining area, we found not an endless panorama but rather a dense fog surrounding us. After taking our seats along the outer perimeter in the slowly rotating dining room, we began our intimate conversation. Just looking at Marilyn was better than any vista from the Skylon. But every once in a while, the fog would open like a crack in a spinster's curtain, and we would be able to see the lights of buildings, car headlights as they moved slowly below us on earth, and even an occasional human figure near a streetlight. It was as if we had transcended our earthly existence and were celestial spirits gazing down on a simple world with minimal, uncomplicated activity.

Our dinner was more fabulous and memorable because of the

special circumstances surrounding us. It was our first major family holiday together, and we had no family rifts to work through. It was just her and me. Our love was evident in everything we said or did, and the outside world was unable to pierce the impenetrable walls of that love. This day was going to be the genesis for the rest of the holidays in our life. There was absolutely no doubt in our minds that the day was the beginning of all the holidays for the rest of our lives together.

After a leisurely dinner of roast turkey, sweet potatoes, carrots, salad, and apple pie à la mode with a simple coffee, we descended back down to earth. We walked in the comforting fog and darkness back to the bus station to catch our Greyhound bus back to downtown Buffalo and the complicated world we had escaped for a precious few hours. The bus, which was all but empty except for the bus driver and us, traveled along the Niagara River on the Canadian side. We held hands as we watched the dreamy images come into and out of our mostly fixed gazes with our heads resting gently against one another. We spoke sparingly, as if we were memorizing everything we were seeing, and as we reflected on all the details of our romantic dinner.

Whenever I spent time with Marilyn, I would feel a sharp sadness grip me once I realized the end of another day with her was approaching. Every single day, I would feel the unique despair of a lover at the impending absence of the beloved. Before long your love would be out of sight, out of physical touch, and only memories would be left to sustain you. If you were lucky, the scent of a trace of her perfume remaining on your clothes and the sensation of her lips upon yours would confirm that you had just ended another precious time together.

After getting Marilyn back home via one Greyhound bus and two city buses, I took the final two city buses back to my home alone. As I stared out the window of the near-empty, bouncing old bus, images of Marilyn dressed in her glamorous green suit, with her long golden hair flowing down her shoulders and her sparkling, intense blue eyes looking lovingly at me, made me both happy and sad at once. I was ecstatic to have just experienced a perfect time together but sad we were not together at the moment of reverie.

Although we had taken many buses and had to walk miles through a mystic fog to get to the Skylon, I would recall the day over and over again throughout my life. Every detail would radiate in my memory and remind me of the power and sanctity of our blossoming, sovereign love. Thanksgiving Day, November 25, 1965, would take its place near the top of the altar of my memories, never to be forgotten and often to be recalled.

A Last Parental Interference/ Our Great Escape

Marilyn had taken a job, as I said earlier, making the minimum wage in an office on the near east side of downtown Buffalo. And as the situation at her home went from contentious to critical, we formulated a plan to free her and to get us together in a significant way. The legal age (that is to say, adulthood in New York State) was eighteen. Once you reached that age, you could assert your rights as an adult. Marilyn would reach that important threshold at the end of December. My time would follow five months later.

At the beginning of December, her parents again tried to interfere with our relationship by telling Marilyn they wanted us to see less of one another. Perhaps they had thought that letting us be together from the end of August would make our love diminish and burn itself out. Just the opposite occurred, and our romance flourished. Their new action to interrupt and possibly end our relationship was a last-ditch attempt at flexing their parental authority over Marilyn and me before she reached legal adulthood.

We knew an open confrontation with her elderly, fixed-thinking father would probably result in greater sanctions and conflict, so we devised a plan for a great escape. We hunted through the want ads of the *Buffalo Evening News* for furnished apartments. One of the ads was for a one-bedroom furnished apartment just a half block away from my high school and six blocks away from my mother's flat. The apartment was located right on the Grant Street bus line, which ended in downtown Buffalo near where Marilyn worked. The bus stop was less than a football field away from the apartment, and the rent was $40 per month, which was exactly one week's gross earnings.

We boldly took the apartment for January 1, 1966. That was the target date because on December 29, Marilyn turned eighteen and formally became a *legal* adult. In order to rent the apartment, we had to tell the landlord we were recently married. One look at us seemed to verify that white lie. It was the goal we both sought, and saying we were married before we actually were, was necessary on many fronts. At that time, if people who weren't married lived together (in so-called sin), they were exposed to an ugly stigma, not to mention a lot of potentially damaging innuendo and venomous gossip. By feigning marriage, we were elevated to a special status: young newlyweds.

After securing the apartment in mid-December, we started smuggling out Marilyn's clothes and portable possessions from her G. Street house. Her parents would never approve of her decision to move out, and we needed to pull off the final phase with the least amount of loose ends. No furniture would be involved, but all of her wardrobe and personal items needed to be transported, a little at a time, so no suspicion would be raised.

We spent Christmas and New Year's around both of our families, and neither side was aware of our secret endeavor. One fateful day during the second week of January, while her father was at work, Marilyn broke the news to her mother, who flew into a rage and pleaded with her to reconsider. But Marilyn would have none of it. She needed to be away from the acrimony and recriminations of her father—and she needed to be with me. Nothing her mother could say or do would change her mind or our plan to be together.

When I showed up to escort Marilyn away from her parents' house, her poor, distraught mother, unable to fathom why her only daughter was seemingly abandoning the family, launched what she thought was the most hurtful thing she could say to me. *"You're a N———!"* she angrily yelled at me from the top stair of her porch. The words bounced harmlessly off me as Marilyn and I headed to the Seneca Street bus stop and the beginning of our life together.

* * *

CHAPTER EIGHT

A Brave New World/Creating Paradise

It had to be
The only one for me is you
And you for me
So happy together ...
From: "Happy Together" by The Turtles

Our second-floor furnished apartment consisted of a small sitting room with a couch, a chair, an end table, a coffee table, and an old black and white television set that received only three precable stations. A small, nondescript oval area rug covered a portion of the wood floor. The quaint eat-in kitchen had a small gas stove, a small table with two chairs, an apartment-sized refrigerator, and some limited cupboard space above a concise sink. The bathroom, at the back of the apartment, consisted of a sink with a medicine cabinet above it, a bathtub, and a commode, all in a maximized space. Our bedroom, in the center of the apartment off the kitchen, contained an end table with a lamp on it, a small closet, a dresser, and a full-sized bed. The apartment was situated on the second floor of a cottage set back from the front house, which was closer to Normal Avenue and just an hundred yards from Grover Cleveland High School.

It became my task to do the grocery shopping, usually at Super Duper Supermarket, where I worked. My cooking skills, still in the embryonic stage, revolved around a lot of meals fried on top of the stove. Marilyn and I ate much of what I call blue-collar fare, like fried peppers, sliced potatoes, and onions with sliced hot dogs. Her expertise was baking. She was a wonderful baker, a skill her mother allowed her to develop at home. Mrs. S. was the exclusive cook of the meals for her family of six. I had found her mother's cooking to be quite good. My Italian palate had been accustomed to the spicy traditional meals of my ancestry, but I recognized good cooking regardless of ethnicity.

However, in our new world together, I took the lead in cooking our weeknight dinners simply because I had more free time than Marilyn. By the time she got home it would be six p.m. and the poor soul was tired, so I wanted to do everything possible to make her life easier. Some people when thrust together seven days a week grow tired of each other and their relationship fizzles. Being together with her every single day never made me tire of her. In fact, the opposite occurred. I could never spend too much time with her or grow tired of seeing her. As proof of this last point, I would take a bus downtown to meet her and ride home with her whenever I wasn't working at the supermarket. John Sebastian and the Lovin' Spoonful had a current song that captured my sentiment perfectly.

My darling be home soon
It's not just these few hours but I've been waiting since I toddled
For the great relief of having you to talk to.
From: "Darlin' Be Home Soon"

Meeting Marilyn as she left work gave us an extra hour to be together. After school I'd catch a bus to downtown Buffalo and go over to the Erie County Public Library and read for about an hour or so. Then I would walk the several blocks to her office to meet her as she left work. When she emerged, we'd passionately embrace and kiss once. Then we would hold hands as we walked to the bus stop three quarters of a mile away to catch the #3 bus back to our apartment. Along the way, we would share the events of our individual days. Our conversation would continue unabated on the bus and then into our apartment. We would eat dinner, usually prepared by me while Marilyn changed her clothes, and afterward relax and unwind watching television.

Since we had been reunited after the motorcycle accident and long, lonely summer, our love had grown tremendously, and both of us continued to feel an absolute certainty about it. Along our journey, our love had blossomed into a full and passionate love that was consummated in the early fall of 1965. Once we began living together in our first apartment, with no worry about privacy, we were able to fully engage our passionate physical love. The relationship I shared with her in my early manhood would dwarf anything I would ever again experience in my life. My love for her was total and complete, and I worshiped everything about her, both intellectually and physically. My love was insatiable, and there was nothing I wouldn't do for her—nothing.

I lived every day as if it was my final day of life. I never missed a moment to be with my love and to express that love for her by holding her hand, embracing her, or kissing her. The joy and fulfillment I felt when I was with her was so powerful and complete, I had a hard time believing I wasn't dreaming. At times, I doubted I was worthy of someone so beautiful, bright, and special. So much in my life before Marilyn had been filled with sadness and darkness. But once she entered my world, her essence purged all the sadness, and light replaced the darkness. Every day, the moment my eyes would see her, my heart would pound, and a wave of euphoria swept through my being. My very life was defined by her existence in it. I felt purpose and meaning, and being with her was the greatest good I had ever known in my short, turbulent life. Nothing and no one was more vital to my existence. She, too, echoed the same passion and commitment toward me.

Building Bridges and Seeking Answers

Our adjustments to this exciting new world we had created were not always easy. She and I were eighteen and seventeen, respectively, and green as far as serious relationships were concerned. Our intense, comprehensive dialogues, along with our ability to express ourselves at great depth, allowed us to learn not only much about one another but also much about ourselves. Communication was a necessary cornerstone to build a lasting relationship. We knew this; most people knew this. As I've said, I was a rational, analytical thinker. My ability to keep my emotions in check at sensitive junctures allowed me to be able to coherently cope with most situations.

Marilyn, too, was analytical and rational. But on occasion, as I would find out, her emotions caused her to become unhinged to the point of crying, sometimes hysterically. At those times, I attempted to understand her pain and to help her see that whatever was causing her such pain could be overcome by us, together, no matter what. Our love could conqueror any problem we'd face. I believed it with every cell in my body.

But sometimes the words I used would not quite articulate the power of the idea I was attempting to convey. Eventually, after she cried and the energy of the emotion was expended, we'd end up wrapped in one another's arms in bed. In repose, with our bodies pressed tightly together, we'd slip into a deep sleep. Whenever I'd stir and recall her pain and sorrow earlier in the evening, I would gently kiss her shoulder, cheek, or neck and feel blessed for having this most extraordinary person in my life. I would then put my arms around her again to let her know I was there, and would always be there, before I'd slip back to sleep.

There were times when I, too, lost control of myself. On one occasion, back in our first few weeks of being allowed by her parents to be together, as I was leaving her house, one of her male school friends arrived to visit her. It was just a friend visiting a convalescing friend. A tidal wave of blinding jealousy roared over my imagination, and I became convinced that this visit was somehow the end for me. As Hillary had thrown me over for someone else a year earlier, I imagined Marilyn was about to send me back to my life before her. I had apocalyptic visions of the world on fire and being destroyed. The intensity of my love for her was so great that even the silly, irrational thought that she'd ever abandon our relationship sent me into the closest vision of hell I had ever seen or felt.

Sometimes when we'd have one of those emotionally charged conversations in our apartment, she would be frustrated and sad, and tears would fall. I tried to talk calmly and rationally with her to allay her sadness. Her comments occasionally brought doubt about so much of what we had together that I'd lose my temper and sometimes exploded. On one such occasion, I was so frustrated that I punched the wall, leaving a fist-sized hole. Anger took its toll on me in those rare outbursts. Invariably, I was upset at my inability to control myself. I hated the poison of those terrible emotions.

We were young and innocent and faced formidable challenges in our world. Although we had some bad times with powerful emotional outbursts, in the end our love triumphed and grew. Could it be that two teenagers could find such a rare, deep, and spiritual love together? What perils lay ahead, and could this exquisite passion survive, prosper, and continue to grow?

As we learn, nothing is more beautiful or difficult in life than to sustain a loving relationship, allowing each partner to mature and grow while reaffirming the pledge of love and commitment to one another every day. Balancing all the various aspects of a dynamic emotional relationship is perhaps the most complex, challenging human experience of all. If each party allows the other to grow and develop in an atmosphere of freedom, security, and nurturing love, then nothing is impossible, and true happiness is assured. This was our goal; this was our holy quest. Mornings we would tell one another, *I love you.* And nightly, before sleep overtook our weary young bodies, we repeated those three holy words: *I love you.* The first and last words we spoke to one another every day were the three greatest words in all language. Those words were our only prayer.

I was a developing man who had witnessed the disintegration of my parents' relationship and marriage. The emotional shrapnel from that conflict indelibly affected every one of my siblings in deep and profound ways. All of us would lead our lives in reaction to the cataclysm of that failed relationship. I solemnly pledged to myself to use my father's poor behavior as the counterexample of what I would be as a man, a husband, and a father.

Marilyn, on the other hand, saw her parents' relationship (which was very different than my parents') as a kind of master/slave relationship. Her mother's passive role was not what she aspired toward. Marilyn's intelligence and questioning nature made her a natural opponent of that kind of relationship and her father. He believed that his longevity and success in his job as a longtime railroad engineer granted him automatic superiority over the women in his family. He wasn't always wrong, and Marilyn wasn't always right. But as much as he lived in a distant past, Marilyn was a person of the present and future.

Often in heated discussions, Mr. S. would make references to obscure music, people, and cultural elements that predated the Great Depression and even World War I. On one such occasion, he dismissed Marilyn's honors class education as inferior to his own education before

World War I. How he came to that conclusion was impossible to say, but casting doubt on one of Marilyn's great accomplishments reaped its intended goal. She went from a state of agitation to one of emotional duress.

One of my objectives was to regularly reassure Marilyn of her superior intelligence. I knew she was an incredibly bright young woman and made every effort to remind her of this. With her in my life, I attempted to hone my ability to communicate at a higher and deeper level. Learning to verbalize in spoken words what our minds were visualizing was of crucial importance to us. In my life, I had never shared such long, rich conversations with anyone else. Although we weren't very old or worldly, our curiosity about life and fascination with those who could express sentiments we felt within was really quite limitless. Our desire to tap into the energy of the life force we felt all around us proved we were kindred spirits. So much was possible; so much amazing life would be ours for the living. The potential was truly unlimited; we felt it, and we lived it. It fueled our happiness.

For several months, our life together meant navigating all sorts of daily obstacles. Every night, as I said, we spent together having dinner and living as if we were a newly married couple. The only thing preventing this was my age. I would turn eighteen on May 7, and we looked forward to formalizing our bond soon afterward. We now had the freedom to express our physical passion, and we did so with deep, loving intensity. Unlike in fleeting teen relationships predicated on an explosive and brief physical interaction, we found ourselves not just intimate but also united spiritually and intellectually. Our combined energy was transcendent, and we reached a state of bliss and tranquility in that amazing time.

We entered sleep every night wrapped in each other's arms, our bodies naked and pure, pressed together in a perfect fusion. In the predawn hours I would stir and then quickly get dressed and return to my mother's apartment. I would clean up and leave for school from there. It was a small concession to her and gave the impression I still lived at home. My poor mother didn't need anybody second-guessing her judgment with regard to me.

I would depart for school from my mother's, and Marilyn would depart from our apartment to go to her job in downtown Buffalo. We passed our days in those two separate roles. At school, my friends and classmates gossiped about teenage stuff like going to parties, hanging out at the pool hall, meeting easy girls, and other such typical teenage activities I came to view as no longer relevant in my life. I was living as a newlywed married man, which was anathema to most of my peers. They didn't know, couldn't know, and probably would never know or achieve as profound an intimacy as I had at that exact time.

The details of my ardent personal life were not shared with any other person. I was all too familiar with how guys spoke about women who had intimately surrendered to adolescent guys they trusted. There was a kind of filthy savagery in their hurtful comments, and those naive, scorned women had to live in constant ridicule and abuse after stories (some exaggerated, some terrible lies) began to circulate about them. They wore a scarlet letter and often were subjected to social and verbal abuse by other teenage women as well.

The thought of anyone saying anything nasty or vile about Marilyn was out of the question. Our life together was a sacred pact of our great love, and I wasn't going to allow anyone to have any idea of its existence, which might create fodder for wicked rumors or vicious comments. Not another soul would be privy to the secret world of love, passion, and happiness we shared as a couple. And as I would learn in the future through reading great literature, few lovers would attain the passion and intimacy we had reached at such a tender age. Shakespeare's Romeo and Juliet came close to what we had actually lived in real life. But without any influence from that story (neither of us had yet read it), we had achieved an intensity and purity that rivaled it in some essential ways.

We had fought many personal and emotional battles in our separate lives before we met and got to the sanctuary in which we found ourselves now living. Our stormy family lives seemed destined to melt into the past and fall away forever. We were creating a world so special and so utterly unique, it made us tremble with excitement. One of the basic principles we established in our all-night discourses, back in the summer of our forced separation, was that we had to be each other's greatest and most trusted friend, someone whom we could always count on completely and totally. We strived to be all things to one another.

Much of our relationship was as perfect as two lovers could humanly achieve together. We shared almost every thought and spoke about all the things happening in our lives. We each offered the other solace and comfort during the rough times and celebrated the good things together. Real communication, talking about all subjects and all the feelings we had about them, was the foundation of our relationship. Our knowledge about one another and ourselves became vast. The more we learned and the more we understood, the more our love intensified. Our views were not identical, and we often approached subjects from widely diverse viewpoints. But no matter what was said, it usually was insightful and intelligent. Both of us recognized perceptive statements, but we also knew we had much to learn about everything.

Our first order of business was to learn as much as possible so we could work tirelessly to create an environment for our love to flourish and grow in all areas. We had mastered speaking our hearts and minds and listening attentively and compassionately to one another. We learned to reason together as almost one focused consciousness. We were young, fearless visionaries in that respect.

Because of my family's implosion, and the subsequent chaos that followed, I had attained a degree of freedom that Marilyn could not achieve living under her father's roof. The direction we were looking to take our lives was beyond the realm of comprehension or tolerance of a man who was born in the nineteenth century and who had graduated from high school before World War I. The rigidity of thinking he possessed made simple discussion impossible. The harrowing arguments at her parents' house had taken a painful toll on that sweet, innocent, fragile soul.

My role became that of rescuing her from the visceral environment laying siege upon her pure, gentle spirit. She, on the other hand, empowered my optimism about life, my sense of happiness, and the sunrise of my manhood. With her in my life, the painful residue of a childhood spent seeing a failed family engulfed in poverty and deprivation on many fronts began to fade like a bad dream in the emerging sunshine of a new day.

Every day with Marilyn, my spirit not only continued to heal from my childhood wounds but soared to heights I never knew existed. Could happiness be this simple? Was love, *real love*, all it took to find inner peace, joy, and boundless happiness? Based upon my conversations with my friends and my observations of everyone around me, I knew that what we had was quite rare and special. I didn't personally know anyone with the same absolute commitment of love and devotion as ours.

Ultimately, it didn't matter what others felt or did. What *we* felt and did, irrespective of the outside world, was all that mattered to us. The intimate details about the inner workings of our relationship remained between us. Advice and counseling from outsiders could never be valid because few people could fathom the depth of love and commitment we had achieved. Few of our friends had the intellectual curiosity we possessed. Most of those around us were caught up in the superficial nature of those turbulent times and lived as most of the world did, which was in a rather myopic, day-to-day existence. They didn't question their world and would end up living very conventional lives eerily similar to the lives of the parents they rebelled against.

At eighteen and seventeen, respectively, Marilyn and I were in uncharted waters. Emotionally, we were reaching an apex. Intellectually, our potential was still in the future. Our capacity to assimilate and develop cognitively continued unimpeded. The variables of life seemed to bombard our burgeoning lives at a frightening pace. We tried to balance our existence amid all the new obstacles arising, which none of our friends were experiencing. We had to pretend we were married, and I was always uncomfortable leaving our apartment in the predawn hours. If I could have had my way, I would never have left. But I had to spare my mother any grief associated with having a *liberated minor*.

Our combined income was meager, but we made do with the dollars we had. Marilyn had a full-time job and paid the rent, which included utilities. I paid for our food, and when the weather broke and I was able to put my motorcycle on the road, we were able to reduce our transportation costs. My part-time job produced a modest income. Some went to help my mother, and whatever was left was used for Marilyn and me in our secluded life. Our life together was filled with so many challenges, it's hard to imagine how our love was able to thrive the way it did. But make no mistake about the enormous sacrifice Marilyn had made for us to be together. She gave up her family, left her world behind, and freely entered my West Side world.

The Gift: A Sacrifice for My Beloved

In those days not every home had a telephone, and we were among those ranks. Communication with Marilyn's few close friends and her brothers, Harry and Jimmy, was quite limited. She gave up everything for me, and I knew it and appreciated it with all my heart. Although I was geographically in the same neighborhood where I had lived before meeting Marilyn, we created a secret island totally invisible to the outside world. She proved her love in every way, every day. On one occasion, in the second month of living together, an opportunity arose for me to do something special for her, something that would give her joy and demonstrate my love and appreciation for all she had sacrificed for me.

Marilyn had a talent for sewing and making clothes. She had a keen eye for style and fashion and always looked sensational no matter what she wore. Since leaving her parents' house, she was deprived of access to a sewing machine and one of her great passions. Our combined income in our first apartment allowed us to cover the basics with only a small amount left over, far too little to entertain the idea of buying a sewing machine.

But one day in February, while listening to the radio, I heard a commercial for the Singer sewing machine store on Main Street in downtown Buffalo. To celebrate President's Day, the store was giving away two sewing machines to the first two people arriving at the store when it opened at nine a.m. This seemed to be a wish come true, and all I had to do was be one of the two lucky people waiting in line when the store opened that day, a school holiday for me. *No problem,* I thought to myself.

I caught the first Grant Street bus on that frigid February morning and was the first person to arrive at the store at about six fifteen a.m. The temperature was in the teens, and winds danced off frozen Lake Erie through the abandoned, gloomy downtown streets. I had several layers of clothing on and was determined to diligently guard my place in line, to get first choice of the two sewing machines to be given away.

The winds hauntingly howled through the dark, desolate streets, racing past lampposts and unlit storefronts with a special ferocity. Downtown Buffalo is situated on the receiving end of the westerly winds that sometimes originate in the Arctic and slice a path all the way to the East Coast and beyond. No object along that path, animate or inanimate, is spared their icy embrace. Even if you wear layer upon layer of clothing, you quickly learn that enough clothing is never enough.

While I stood in line, with little ability to warm myself by engaging in any real physical activity other than shuffling my fast-numbing feet and opening and closing my hands rapidly, I found myself getting colder and colder. The prospect of staying in one spot for nearly three hours, with the wind chill dropping to a frightening and dangerous level, began to call into question the prudence of my goal. I had made up my mind to be the first in line to get that sewing machine for Marilyn, and I did not seriously consider surrendering my prize place in line. A high physical price would have to be paid, and I was bound and determined to pay it.

For about an hour and a half, the winds continued to slash away at my body. My feet were so cold that I couldn't feel my toes, which I futilely tried to wiggle in a vain effort to keep warm. My fingers, hiding in my gloves, buried in my pea coat pockets, and tightly pressed against my torso, were throbbing. Clearly, I had vastly underestimated the impact of the frigid temperature and wicked winds, especially when I would be essentially stationary for nearly three interminably long hours.

My resolve was called into question, but my determined goal overrode any thought of retreat. The minutes seemed to drag, and pain started emanating from my extremities. I tried to banish the thought of what my poor hands and feet were feeling by the thought of how happy this mysterious sewing machine would make Marilyn. Imagining the joy and purpose she would get from being able to sew again became the only thought I would allow my mind to focus on. With that image in my mind, my resolve resurged. Nothing and no one could force me from my prime place in line or my goal to provide Marilyn with this special gift. Daylight began to vanquish the darkness, but the winds continued to punish my painfully chilled body.

By the time the store opened, several other people had arrived to compete for the second prize. Others arrived and quickly left, knowing the math was not in their favor: three to infinity equals nothing. Once the door of the store was unlocked, my torso carried my hands and pushed my feet into the welcoming warmth of the showroom. I was led by the manager to an area where two used portable sewing machines were displayed and given first choice between them. I chose the White sewing machine because it appeared to be of better quality. Obviously these were trade-ins, but it didn't matter to me as long as Marilyn was able to express her skill with one and feel some joy.

After a few minutes of absorbing some resuscitating warmth and feeling my toes and fingers aroused from their frigid coma, I carried my treasure off to Shelton Square to catch the #3 Grant Street bus back to our simply furnished apartment. I set the machine up for Marilyn to see when she came home from work at the end of the day. I knew the joy she'd feel when she saw it and that would make the pain I had endured to win it worthwhile. She'd never know the full extent of how much pain it had caused me to stand in the brutal elements for nearly three hours, nor would she know how much joy it gave me to see her smile when we got home at dinner time. It was a sacrifice that an affluent person would never endure or understand. But, most importantly, it was a demonstration of selfless true love.

I was never big on fanfare, nor did I need much more than a simple thank-you. The smile on her face that arctic day was my reward, and recalling it more than four decades later proves that my modest sacrifice was worth it. Her smile was worth any sacrifice I could make, and the thought of it brings an ancient joy to my heart.

Desperately Searching for Permanent Solutions

During those first intense months of living together, our youthfulness and lack of emotional maturity worked against us at times. There were so many moments when words failed me and I would be unable to breach one of the emotional crevasses that would appear in our path. An argument might arise, and, with the failure of language and experience, we would be unable to communicate clearly or compromise on a position. Too often, Marilyn shed tears and expressed hurt and pain. In those sad moments, I found myself feeling like a failure and less of a man than I wanted to be. I am haunted by the sound of her weeping and the image of tears falling from those exquisitely beautiful eyes. There were forces at play that my youthful innocence and immaturity were ill equipped to handle. None of my friends ever spoke of moments like this, and, of course, I could not solicit advice on a topic so alien to their experience.

I believed all problems and situations could be successfully overcome by using disciplined logic and reason. Simply identifying all the various elements of a particular issue and then systematically analyzing options to remedy the problem was my modus operandi. But adding fiery emotions into the equation produced a far more complex dilemma than my still maturing, but willing, mind was equipped to handle. Marilyn had deep pockets of emotion that seemed resistant to my earnest but rather simplistic approach to problem solving. These temporary impasses proved quite frustrating, but they almost always passed without long-term residual effect. It was impossible to say exactly what triggered these painful episodes, but they appeared only occasionally.

In my naiveté, I hoped they'd simply vanish on their own or that somehow I could find a permanent resolution to alleviate them forever. I was innocently ignorant of erratic mood swings in general, and menstrual cycle mood swings in particular. Although I had grown up in a house with four females, I was never given any information about such things. If one of my older sisters acted overly emotional, it was explained in a way that kept me clueless regarding the real reason for it. Some men believed that a man must impose a dominant presence during difficult emotional times, treating the woman as a subordinate, an inferior, a possession. That sort of mind-set was archaic, crude, and wrong. And I rejected such a chauvinistic position outright. I wanted to understand the cause so I could find a lasting solution.

A Hint of Spring and Rebirth Again

Months passed living on Normal Avenue with Marilyn working downtown and me attending Grover Cleveland High and working at Super Duper. When March 1 arrived, I put my Yamaha back on the road, although consistently good weather, drivable weather, was still weeks away. But having the option to drive my motorcycle when the opportunity arose greatly enhanced our ability to break through our indoor humdrum winter confinement.

There were some days when it was sunny but quite cold. We would dress with layers of clothes and wear gloves to venture off on our remarkably reliable Yamaha. The air was so cold, sometimes in the twenties, that it made our eyes tear. We didn't go very far or for very long, but it gave us hope for the inevitable beautiful, warm spring weather that would be upon us soon. There is a special magic and excitement in the air when spring arrives in the Northeast. The sound of birds singing, the appearance of flowers and growing vegetation, the smell of grass, and the medicinal warmth of sunlight on bare flesh stir our hearts and souls from wintry hibernation. Our spirits feel an enhanced, energized transfusion of life, and the days grow longer.

In this environment of nature awakening, we found ourselves spending every joyful day together, looking forward beyond daily survival toward the future. Our plan to marry and move to California, where I would attend the business college I had applied to, was up in the air until I received formal notification of my acceptance. My application for summer employment at Bethlehem Steel in Lackawanna would also be accepted soon. There had been promises of a great income working in the antiquated steel mill.

Amid the changing seasons, we decided to leave our first apartment and move to another apartment closer to Super Duper and my mother's apartment. The one-year-old Yamaha had a remarkable eleven thousand kilometers on it after about ten months of driving, so I decided it was time for an upgrade. We went to Imperial Cycle on Michigan Avenue and met the owner, Gus. I ended up purchasing a used CB160 Honda that was two years old and in mint condition. It had been owned by a friend of mine from Super Duper who had traded it in. Joe had chromed both front and back fenders, and it looked great.

I got a loan from my credit union and traded in my well-traveled Yamaha for the black and chrome Honda. Marilyn and I picked it up on a chilly April afternoon and immediately took it to the Scajaqueda Expressway to give it a test run. The swift motorcycle quickly reached the highway speed limit, and our eyes watered from the rush of cold air. Both of us were impressed with its greater power, its heavier weight, and its improved comfort. It would open new possibilities and help to expand our circle of activities.

Because of the increased weight of the motorcycle, I would be able to drive more safely on faster roadways. Things seemed to be looking up, but new challenges and more unanticipated obstacles were just ahead, like the unexpected approach of storm clouds on a summer's day.

All the leaves are brown and the sky is grey
I've been for a walk on a winter's day I'd be safe and warm if I was in LA
California dreaming on such a winter's day ...
From: "California Dreamin'" by The Mamas and the Papas

* * *

Chapter Nine

An Olive Branch from a Past World

The end of my high school days approached with the prospect of college beginning to materialize. Since my relationship began with Marilyn, my connection to my high school had become tenuous and, at best, superficial. I couldn't wait to begin an exciting new chapter of my life with my love. High school in some real way was linked to my childhood. My relationship with Marilyn represented and cultivated my manhood. Shedding my time at Grover was the final stage of my metamorphosis into manhood. Although I had many friends and memories there, the chapter would end none too soon for my soaring spirit.

Originally, we had planned to move to California, where I would attend college and work. I applied for and was accepted to Woodbury Business School in Los Angeles. The thought behind it was that I could get a business degree and find a decent job out West. Neither of us had a clue as to the actual cost of such an education, not to mention the cost of living in Southern California. We had blind faith that it would all work out.

As time passed and graduation approached in June, something unexpected happened. Marilyn's mother contacted her by telephone at work and offered her an opportunity to move back home. We were told that her parents had come to their senses and realized our relationship was for real, not just a passing fancy between two love-struck teenagers. The olive branch seemed genuine and sincere. By moving back home, Marilyn could save much of the money she earned, and she'd be able to have the freedom she didn't have before she moved out.

I was going to be working full-time at Bethlehem Steel Mill on the swing shift. Having Marilyn move back to her family home would allow both of us to save more money and, I thought, provide her with some basic family support and, more importantly, female emotional comfort, which I clearly couldn't provide. Coincidentally, Marilyn was able to find a better paying job at Buffalo General Hospital as a receptionist in the X-ray department.

In late June, the week following my graduation, I began work at Bethlehem Steel in Lackawanna. The job paid a whopping $2.385 per hour, which was nearly double the new minimum wage of $1.25 per hour. Unfortunately, I was placed on a thirty-two hour per week schedule, which reduced my potential earnings by twenty percent. After taxes my take-home check was a mere sixty-six dollars per week. My goal of amassing a large surplus of money for our initial plan fell far short. Prospects for going to LA went from slim to none; we needed to regroup and come up with a viable alternative plan.

Since it was now virtually impossible to apply for the fall semester at a local college, I decided to apply for admission for spring semester at Buffalo State, the teacher's college. The idea of a business degree gave way to a plan for me to teach high school, a vocation many of my teachers had urged me to pursue. By doing this, I would be able to continue working at the steel mill in the fall and could actually find a part-time second job.

Having Marilyn living with her parents at home helped her out financially, and it gave me a certain peace of mind to know that she would not be alone in a small furnished apartment while I was working on the swing shift. With the tenure in the second furnished apartment drawing to a close, I began to realize how our young lives were again going to be challenged by distance and absences.

As trying as our intense months living together had been in those occasional moments, the thought of not sleeping together, wrapped tenderly in each other's arms every night, depressed me. Not being able to find my true love next to me in the middle of the night, when my regular and vivid dreams often awakened me, deeply saddened me. The plans we had made in order to be able to move forward to accomplish our revised plan for the future allowed both of us to take our new roles in stride, although we were sad about the prospect of not sleeping in one another's arms at night.

Summer of Sun, Sand, and Fun/Autumn of Changes, Challenges, and New Problems

Sunshine came softly through my a-window today
Could've tripped out easy but I've a-changed my ways
It'll take time, I know it but in a while
You're gonna be mine, I know it, we'll do it in style
'Cause I made my mind up you're going to be mine.

Sunshine Superman
Written by Donovan Leitch
Copyright 1966 Donovan (Music) Ltd.

This new arrangement worked out wonderfully, at first. I usually had one or both weekend days off from the steel mill, and Marilyn worked steady days, Monday through Friday. When the weather cooperated (which it almost always did in the summer of 1966), we would be off to Bay Beach in Canada. We spent the whole time swimming and sunning. Riding on our CB160 Honda was terrific. On Saturdays, after the beach, we often drove to Joe Martucci's pizzeria on Walden and Bailey Avenue for a pizza. A large cheese and pepperoni pizza was $2.08. We'd also pick up a couple bottles of Orange Crush with it and drive back to Marilyn's parents' house to share our meal with any of her family members who might be home. Afterward, we'd watch television, and I'd usually leave at eleven p.m. or so to go back to my mother's apartment on the West Side. The next morning I'd return to Marilyn's house to pick her up for an encore visit to Bay Beach.

Over the summer we bought two rubber air mattresses that were portable enough to transport along with the other modest beach gear we carried on our Honda. Of course, I was in charge of inflating our mattresses, which allowed us to float out from the crowded beach into peaceful deeper water. We were like two innocent children enjoying the simple pleasures of a beautiful beach with our closest friend. Everything was uncomplicated and natural; maybe that's why it was so much fun and so wonderful. By end of the summer, both of us were tanned, relaxed, and, for the most part, feeling that the new living arrangement was working.

Back at the steel mill, I made my intention clear: I would not be leaving after Labor Day with the rest of the *white hats* (the color of helmet worn by the temporary summer workers, who were mostly college students on break) to return to college. I had established myself as a tireless hard worker who handled any task without complaint. Joe T., the assistant superintendent of the mill, liked my positive attitude and work ethic, so he helped me in my effort to keep working past summer. He even arranged for me to work steady nights (eleven p.m. to seven a.m.). This was no small favor because it freed me from the roulette of the swing shift.

I eventually found out that few foremen worked the night shift, and the workload and expectations were greatly reduced. Once you completed your tasks as defined by the foreman on the shift, you were free to engage in other nonwork-related activities, but sleeping was considered a dismissible activity and strongly discouraged. My coworkers read tabloid newspapers, played cards, made small talk, and generally killed off the free hours handed to them on a golden platter. For the first time, I now had a substantial block of free time without real distraction to use as I pleased.

I decided it was the perfect opportunity to launch into some serious reading. It was the fall of 1966, most of my friends were in college or going into the armed services, and I was anxious to begin my higher education. I recalled many comments from my favorite English teacher from my senior year at Grover and some of Marilyn's suggestions. I plunged into an intense period of voracious reading. First I devoured *Lord of the Flies, Brave New World*, and *1984*; then I jumped into a series of works by Fyodor Dostoevsky: *Poor Folk, House of the Dead, The Gambler, The Brothers Karamazov, Crime and Punishment*, and a tale that turned me on my head and caused me to hit an intellectual brick wall—*Notes from Underground*.

I had read *Crime and Punishment* with great eagerness and found myself mesmerized by Rascolnikov's vision of the world and his plight to survive in it. I identified with his struggle as an outsider and the bleak world he faced. It amazed me how my life in the twentieth century had parallels to the character in the pages of a novel written by a Russian in the nineteenth century. It was like I was tasting filet mignon after a lifetime of eating gruel. The intellectual surge I began to experience made me realize the special gift I had within me to connect with the life force of a world created in a great novel of world literature. It made me aware of the vast inner world that existed within my mind and spirit, and it inspired a driving desire to delve deeper.

A couple of things occurred as a result of my intense submersion into Dostoevsky's works. I thought I comprehended everything I had read with the exception of one work: *Notes from Underground*. It was alien to my experience and understanding of human nature at that point in my intellectual development. Formal existential philosophy hadn't entered my awareness yet, and I intuitively felt that this work was something I would have to return to once I had reached a higher stratum of consciousness in the future.

Reading Dostoevsky also heightened my sensitivity to the suffering and peril people face in life. I realized that anyone's life could be transformed with a single devastating occurrence. During parts of some days when I wasn't working, I often went to bookstores in downtown Buffalo to search for more reading material. You could easily see panhandlers bouncing from pedestrian to pedestrian trying to get handouts along Main Street. When I would see those ragtag, usually unshaven, glossy-eyed beggars, I would think to myself: *That could happen to anyone, including me, if certain tragic events befell them.*

I knew that whatever money was given to them was often converted into booze or drugs. I wanted to help, but I didn't want to enable a drinking or drug habit. So when someone approached me to get money for coffee or food, I would take them to one of the many restaurants along Main Street and buy them a meal. I'd sit with them and listen to their unique story, and then I would offer whatever heartfelt advice my optimistic, innocent mind could muster.

After reading Dostoevsky, I would never be the same. My feeling for people who suffered would be forever heightened. The sense of desolation felt by the characters in Dostoevsky's works, and the insurmountable and inscrutable circumstances that they faced, left an indelible imprint upon me. No matter how good or privileged our life was, we were one occurrence away from the fate some of Dostoevsky's characters faced. Their suffering, although on the pages of his works, was as real to me as the people I worked with in the Lackawanna labyrinth. What I saw, what I perceived, what I believed, was that life is, at best, *tenuous*. Whatever joy and happiness we enjoyed, we must savor it, for in an instant it could be gone.

Self-Discovery, Death, and a Renewed Rift

I's taught and brought up there
The laws to abide
And the land that I live in
Has God on its side.
From: "With God on Our Side" by Bob Dylan

When I was eighteen years old, my mind began accelerating to another plateau. In my real world, caskets with young people I knew came home from Vietnam, racism and its hideous outlets were everywhere, and friends and acquaintances of my generation were under enormous pressure to participate in the absurdity of a jungle war. Truth was under siege, actively being warped to fit the needs of what appeared to me to be the rich and powerful. The world we found ourselves in had begun to seriously nullify whatever idyllic illusions remained from childhood. We found ourselves in deadly times, and we were being told we had to participate in unquestioning silence.

During the fall of 1966, while I was working full time at Bethlehem Steel, I was classified 1-A with the draft board, which meant that my exposure was at the highest degree of the military draft. Until I was formally registered for classes, I could be drafted and sent to the Southeast Asian jungles. I was in grave jeopardy, and there was nothing to do but keep working and hoping I didn't hear from the draft board before I registered for classes at Buffalo State College, where I was accepted for spring 1967. Registration was in January, and all I could do was trust that the draft board bureaucracy was as inefficient as the rest of its governmental counterparts.

The thought of being drafted and taken away from Marilyn began to cross my mind. We watched news reports about the war on television and read about it in the *Buffalo Evening News* and in magazines, and we kept hearing the conflicting stories from actual participants. They would do pieces on the nightly news extolling how superior our brave men were compared to the seemingly mysterious enemy who were everywhere and yet nowhere. Our side was bombing and killing tremendous numbers of the enemy, but curiously, when it was all said and done, the enemy's numbers weren't noticeably decreased, and our generals requested another increase in our troop level—which was never questioned. According to the confusing reports, we were winning, but the enemy didn't seem to be losing. There was something very odd occurring, and nobody could coherently explain it. Questions and doubts began to arise.

During the autumn, before I was safely registered for classes, I had a disturbing dream full of nightmare images and a vision that I couldn't explain but was scorched in my mind. I dreamt I was in Shea's Buffalo Theater, chained ankle and wrist to someone in front of me and someone behind me. There were two aisles leading down to where the stage and screen should be, but instead of the regular stage and screen, there was a large open-hearth furnace like I'd see at Bethlehem Steel every workday. After the person closest to the open door and horrific heat jumped into the flames, our whole line was dragged closer to the intense, glowing heat. Every new first person in the front of both lines would stand there in the stifling, scalding heat for a few minutes until the heat grew so unbearable that he would leap through the furnace threshold, to where the incinerated remains of the previous person lay smoldering, to end his own agonizing pain. Once another young man fed the insatiable flames, our lines were jerked forward, one person closer to the next fiery death. I awoke in a sweat, still feeling the horror of seeing one young man after another burning to death as I was pulled closer to my own death. The fatalistic vision, and the fear I felt from it, would remain with me for my entire life.

If I had heard from the draft board at that time, I would've gone voluntarily. But a year later, after many personal conversations with friends and acquaintances who had been in the war, and based on many troubling articles about the Vietnam War in the underground press,

I would've resisted. Once you know the truth, it becomes impossible to participate in a lie. And Vietnam was one of the great lies of the 1960s.

As time passed and the seasons moved from summer into autumn, Marilyn's situation at her parent's house again grew less stable. The old personality conflicts and battle of wills between her father and her intensified. It was just like old times—bad old times, unfortunately. The emotional cost began to mount, and remaining in that environment would take a fearful toll on her. Who wants to argue every single day? Who wants to be questioned about their every action and move? Clearly, it was a critically bad situation that would worsen again with time.

In order to save Marilyn from this progressively terrible situation, my mother graciously offered her a temporary refuge in our compact family apartment. But this arrangement proved to be impractical given the limited space and number of people (six) in the apartment. A short time after Marilyn moved in, a divorced woman friend of my mother, who lived nearby, offered Marilyn a place for her to stay for room and board. This was also a short-term answer as well, and the search for a better answer was somewhat complicated by my acceptance to college, which would begin in mid-January.

In December, through the encouragement of Jack S., a friend from the steel mill, I took a second job, working part time at the *Buffalo Evening News*. The position was as a hopper on a truck distributing bundles of newspapers between two thirty p.m. and six thirty p.m., Monday through Saturday. My work schedule was increased to sixty-four hours per week (forty at Bethlehem Steel and twenty-four at the *Buffalo Evening News*).

Our plan to get married was on hold because of the uncertainty about my impending college career. We weren't expecting me to be able to work a job once I started college, so we planned to reduce the financial burden by having me live at my mother's. My income would drop significantly once I began my full-time academic schedule, and so I decided to try to accumulate as much money as I could beforehand.

With two jobs, I began to temporarily earn a fairly good income for an eighteen-year-old. I had learned to live frugally, but for Christmas I bought my mother her very first brand new, higher-end washer and dryer to make her life better. It gave me so much joy to make her life easier, and she always treasured any gesture, no matter how big or small. That same Christmas, I purchased an exquisite music box for Marilyn. It played "Lara's Theme" from the current romantic movie *Dr. Zhivago* and cost me one week's pay. The movie was released at the time my lifelong love of Russian literature began, and I felt that my love and passion for Marilyn were as great as those of Yury for Lara in Boris Pasternak's novel.

When the weather turned really ugly, my motorcycle couldn't be used. Since there was no bus service to the steel mill, I would hitchhike there at night and home in the morning. This expanded my work night because I needed to allow for the time it would take to catch a friendly ride. During this period of prosperity, I decided I needed to buy my first car. I wasn't interested in a conventional car and wanted something that would be an upgrade from my motorcycle but still be fun. Riding my motorcycle in cold weather and rain was just too painful, and it was impossible when it snowed.

About the time I was looking ahead to my academic life and mentally preparing myself for all the changes on the horizon, a friend of mine approached me about buying his three-year-old 1963 Triumph Spitfire. It was British racing green with a tan leather interior and captured my imagination. It was December, school would be starting in another month, and spring was only a couple of months after that, so I paid cash for the car and stored it for the winter.

* * *

CHAPTER TEN

==

A Miscalculation, Consequences, and Confusion

When college classes began, instead of quitting my all-night job at the steel mill, I foolishly decided to try to continue to work there, attend full-time classes, and keep my part-time job at the *News*. On paper it was a terrific plan: classes from eight a.m. to one p.m., part-time job from two thirty p.m. to six thirty p.m., and full-time job from eleven p.m. to seven a.m. My thought was that I could catch some sleep before my night shift at the steel mill and I'd be able to do some of my serious studying at the steel mill at night. On the two nights a week when I wasn't working at the steel mill, I could catch up on my studying and sleep. Like all well-intentioned idealistic plans, when confronted by harsh reality, this one soon ended up on the rocks.

After three weeks of attempting to manage that three-ring circus, plus maintain my relationship with Marilyn, I began to feel massive fatigue and exhaustion. My indefatigable confidence started to crumble. The physical challenges were being met, for the most part. I had the muscular strength to move hundreds of bundles of newspapers on and off my truck every day at my job at the *News*. I still was able to sweep floors or perform whatever task was given me on the night shift at the steel mill. But when it came to sitting still and reading and absorbing the pages of the diverse books I was required to read for my various college courses, I was in big trouble. Textbooks filled with statistics and rather dry information were a far cry from great novels. Even sitting in my classes during the daytime, I fought to keep from slipping into sleep.

The fear of running out of money kept pushing me. I futilely tried to rally all my energy to meet my many obligations.

By March, my second full month of my Sisyphean routine, it became clear that my academics were in poor shape and I was at risk of possibly flunking out of college. Physically, I began having whole-body spasms when I started dozing off, which would happen anytime, day or night, when my body wasn't moving. Sleep deprivation had begun to exact a price. Clearly, I would have to change what I was doing or risk jeopardizing my college career. I had begun to realize this and knew I wasn't being the man I needed to be to ensure the success of all the adjustments both Marilyn and I were facing. And this overzealous effort to continue working two jobs and trying to succeed in school might threaten our relationship.

Along the way, Marilyn had made friends with an X-ray technician whose name was Ellen Jo. If I knew her last name, it has long since been banished from my memory. She had, I believe, some sort of a birth defect that caused her to walk with a noticeable limp. She was very plain looking with listless brown hair and was about five or six years older than Marilyn. During the time of the turmoil we were going through in late fall and the early winter, Ellen Jo began to influence some of Marilyn's thinking. As I would learn later, there was a hidden agenda at work that would have a devastating impact upon my life.

Around the time I realized I was seriously faltering in school, I was fortuitously laid off from the steel mill but continued to work my part-time job at the *Buffalo Evening News*. I made a concerted effort to salvage my first semester. In a short time, with the aid of sleeping normally in my own bed at night, I began getting *it* at school. What had looked like inevitable disaster at college ended up being a decent turnaround. The road I had been on would have resulted in failing most of my classes and, ultimately, being forced from school and vulnerable to the military draft. Instead, I was able to pass all my courses: medieval history, sociology, English, and philosophy. The latter two courses, which captured my imagination, would influence my academic direction. The former two courses, although I found them quite interesting, held no future direction for me.

Marilyn was graciously invited to share an apartment with Ellen Jo on Linwood Avenue on the upper West Side of Buffalo. She would live there for a few months before again trying to return to her family home. At one point, while Marilyn was living with Ellen Jo, she conveyed to me an opinion Ellen Jo had expressed that should've alarmed me more than it did at the time. She told Marilyn it was common for men to go through college with the help and support of their girlfriends or wives, only to cast them off as they began their professional lives after graduation. I remember dismissing this notion as having no validity whatsoever with regard to me. I couldn't imagine how Marilyn could even listen to such rubbish. I looked deeply into Marilyn's eyes and said: "How could you possibly think such a thing about *me*?" Her eyes dropped in slight shame.

A noticeable drift between us had begun. The more I engaged in academic work, the more our relationship seemed to disconnect. Back home with her family, Marilyn's relationship with her father resumed being unsavory and contentious. The battle of the nineteenth century versus the twentieth century raged on. The life Marilyn came from was in direct conflict with the life she was moving toward. It wasn't about me; it was about the future. And it was crystal clear that reconciliation with her parents could never take place under their roof.

She and I had arguments about, too often, silly or trite things. So much energy was wasted in verbal skirmishes about petty and puny matters. I often found myself wondering how we could engage in such hurtful and painful discussions about nothing at all. After spending time together, I would drive home with my head pounding with the sound of words that had been shot at me. Our discussions turned into arguments and then quickly deteriorated into personal attacks against me. I felt as though I was being placed in the same category as her parents, especially her father, and I did not understand how this could be. She seemed to be trying to alienate me, and I was hurt and confused. My world was spinning wildly, and I was faced with ridiculous challenges. Yet through it all, my love for Marilyn still remained the one pure joy of my life and was the one essential element for any real happiness.

Foregone Conclusions Jeopardized

All my academic life my mother was approached by teachers who told her I was an exceptional student, a gifted child. At one point, my first high school English teacher came to our house unannounced. When I opened the door of our School Street apartment and saw Mr. B., I was transformed into a statue with an open mouth. My mother saw me staring motionless at the tall man, who had a curious resemblance to Abe Lincoln. She gently moved me aside, realizing I was unable to respond politely. Mr. B. sat at our kitchen table with my mother. She gave him a cup of coffee, and he explained who he was and why he decided to visit our home.

For half an hour he spoke about me. He wanted to talk to her and my absent father about my abilities and what he felt was needed so I could keep developing. He asked her about the books we had in the house, and when my mother mentioned my father's detective novels and her biographies of Hollywood movie stars, he urged her to get me *great* books of literature. I was so embarrassed by his compliments that I wanted to hide under my bed.

My whole life, I loved going to school and learning. Everything about it fascinated me, and I could recall almost everything. My power of observation, if it wasn't photographic, was close. There was no doubt in my mind that education would always be a substantial part of my world. Going to college, a place nobody in my entire extended family had attended, was inevitable. I knew it, and everyone expected me to do well. It was a foregone conclusion.

So in my first semester of college, as I tried to work two jobs, attend classes full time, and maintain my relationship with Marilyn, failure seemed all but certain. Once I was laid off from the steel mill and able to concentrate on school, the impact was immediate. As I said, I started getting it, and, more importantly, understood that I had the ability to do well in school—if I made the time. Unlike in grade school and high school, where you can do well by just being attentive in class with little home study, college disproportionately required studying outside of class.

While I was going through all my struggles with working and school and the pressure of the draft hovering over my life like a vulture circling an ailing gazelle, Marilyn was in her personal struggle with her family. She clearly loved her family, especially her brothers, Harry and Jimmy. She loved her mother, too, but when her father turned hostile, her mother always remained on his side. How many times had she tried to make peace and to return home?

She always knew I loved her completely and was her soul mate. But with the beginning of my freshman year and the difficulty I had with working too much and adjusting to *real* studying, she probably felt somewhat abandoned. Whenever we got together, I would excitedly tell her about some of the great lectures I had attended. I wanted her to be a part of the academic world that was capturing my imagination. Our two lives were complicated, and our separate challenges weighed heavily upon our young minds. No clear-cut answer lay in the offing.

A Family Conflict Laid to Rest/ Petty Jealousies Arise

In the fall of 1966, my mother decided to move from Fargo Avenue to a new apartment that was a little smaller, nicer, and less expensive on Niagara Street. A few months into our tenure there, a surprise development took place. After more than six years of estrangement, my grandfather came to his senses and contacted my mother and Aunt Angie. He wanted to make things right with the family. Both daughters were given properties in the Allentown section of Buffalo, and a long, terrible family feud was laid to rest.

My mother's mom, my grandmother, had died in April 1959. My grandfather, who was the pure brawn of that relationship, was quite lost without my grandmother's business acumen and savvy. He found himself not only having to do all the maintenance on their six properties but also wrestling with the foreign paperwork. For my grandfather, who spoke extremely broken English, this was beyond tedious, so my mother and Aunt Angie pitched in with his financial paperwork and the simple domestic tasks my late grandmother had done when she was alive.

It was agreed that my family (my parents and the five children) would move from one of the smaller flats owned by my grandparents into their old residence on Efner Street, the one my mother had lived in before marrying my father. Shortly after we moved in, less than a year after my grandmother's death, a shock wave hit our family: the marriage of my grandfather to an old widow from the Lakeview Housing Project. She was a Sicilian from his old village of Agrigento. My grandfather's loneliness and helplessness with foreign paperwork and domestic skills like cooking and housekeeping had driven him into a rash union with a woman who seemed by all evidence to be a plotting opportunist.

She tried to step right into the role of our family matriarch. It was clear that my mother and her siblings would have no part of this. The many grandchildren saw this woman as an intruder in our grandmother's home. She began to influence my grandfather's thinking and to act as a potent poison in our passionate family chemistry. Arguments began, terrible words were exchanged, and feelings were hurt.

Then two major events occurred that sealed the fate of our family. The pretending matriarch, who had been introducing her relatives into my grandfather's world, started wearing jewelry and clothing that had belonged to my late grandmother. This opened deep emotional wounds. Seeing those extremely personal items on anyone other than my late grandmother created unbearable pain. Tensions increased, and arguments took place daily. My grandfather was, perhaps, too pragmatic. He saw those objects, clothes and jewelry, as external objects with no sentimental value. The sisters saw those objects as extremely personal and intimately connected to the spirit of my late grandmother. The act of wearing them in front of our family was, in effect, an act of denial or an overt attempt to eradicate the memory of my grandmother. The sisters and family were outraged.

While we were living in my grandparent's former residence, my father had taken a job as a bartender, effectively ending his effort to work in construction and *legitimate* industries. It would be during this time that he would make the acquaintance of a woman named Nina, the divorced mother of four children living in the same housing project where my grandfather's second wife had lived. She was a tall, slightly attractive Italian American woman who would begin the process of displacing my mother and our family from my father's life.

My father's behavior grew more erratic, and he began to shirk his responsibilities to our family. He used some of the money he earned to cabaret or party with Nina. My mother's life grew progressively worse. On the one hand, she had her father betraying her mother's memory; on the other hand, she had my father betraying his wedding vows to her. Paying the household bills became more and more difficult. My grandfather's rent was always late. On the advice of his scheming, coldhearted second wife, we were told by my grandfather we must move out. Our grandfather, who neither liked nor trusted my father, made it clear that our problems were *our* problems and we had to get out. Whatever family unity had existed was shattered. Hard feelings, not to mention alienation, were all that remained.

For the next six years, a gulf existed between my grandfather and all of his descendants. No attempt was made to breach it. The immediate first four years after my family was exiled from Efner Street, my mother had to struggle with the lies and subterfuge created by my father. Numerous times he denied there was anything to his wayward behavior and mysterious absences, and he always promised my mother he would change for the better. Time after time my father made empty promises to my mother. In August 1964, the end of my parents' twenty-two-year marriage arrived in one last, great spasm. My father was forever banished from our family life after my mother was secretly informed of my father's mistress's second pregnancy by him.

Late in 1966, my seventy-eight-year-old grandfather reached out to my mother and Aunt Angie, his two closest daughters. He had had a major change of heart and wanted to make things right. He gave my mother the College Street cottage my grandparents had lived in at the time of my grandmother's death. Once a picture-perfect cottage with a striking flower garden and a newly built two-car garage, it had been beaten down by a series of uncaring renters. Aunt Angie received the other two College Street properties, a double in front and a single structure in the rear, located next door to my mother's property. Perhaps sensing his own mortality and needing to be near his descendants, my grandfather stepped up to do the right thing.

With the exception of my oldest sister, Pat, who was already married, our family moved into the College Street cottage just after the start of my first semester of college. We discovered that the house paled by comparison to the home we remembered from many family holidays. It hadn't been painted inside or outside in a long, long time. Many elements were broken and hadn't been fixed in years. Damaged window screens, broken railings, damaged stairs, and many other imperfections hadn't been addressed in ages. My grandfather couldn't keep up with the many repairs and simple upkeep as he used to do when my grandmother was alive, so the house became noticeably run down.

As children, we played in the yard and were always careful not to go near my grandmother's wonderfully diverse flower garden. The outside of the house was always freshly painted, and my grandfather's handmade picket fence always wore a fresh coat of paint. You never saw peeling paint or a broken picket.

Inside the house, my grandmother had acquired and collected numerous porcelain knickknacks, many handmade doilies she had expertly crocheted herself, and a wide assortment of dreaded breakables. All the furniture, from the couch and chairs in the living room to the end tables and Persian area rugs, were older but in museum quality condition. The many little boys in our family viewed the interior of Grandma's house with respect and fear. It was impossible to play any of our favorite active physical games without unsettling the perfectly stationed pieces of furniture and omnipresent knickknacks. To disturb anything or, God forbid, break any of the fragile pieces was to incur the wrath of two generations plus be embarrassed in front of a peanut gallery of nearly two dozen cousins. The house, outside and in, radiated a sense of care and order. Every facet was simple and exact, and it was pristine in every way. That was then.

My mother made some attempts to repair and upgrade the house, but it wasn't possible to pay for the long list of needed items on her meager income. My mother's brother Jim, the youngest of her five brothers, tried to shore up some of the structural problems in the late spring of 1967 during the first few months we lived there.

An ugly episode occurred during this effort that opened my eyes to some petty jealousies and resentment of my attempt to break the mold of my family by going to college. My uncle, with the help of my younger brother Al, was adding a support beam in the living room on the first floor. A sag had developed in the ceiling, and it was necessary to install a long support beam to reinforce and straighten it. Plaster was opened up along the path where the beam was to be placed. Both my uncle and brother were demeaning my academic effort and told my mother that I should be helping them because it just wasn't right for me to be trying to study in my nearby bedroom while they were doing all the *real* work on the ceiling. The two of them were trying to turn my mother against me and were taunting and trying to belittle my attempt to salvage my first semester of college.

I could see what they were doing and decided to make an effort to pitch in as a gesture to my mother. A scaffold had been set up, which my uncle and brother stood on. They were chipping plaster along the path where the support beam was going to be placed. Large plastic buckets were catching chunks of plaster as it was broken away from the ceiling. They had me standing below them on the floor and were handing me buckets of debris that I was taking outside and dumping into a garbage can. My uncle and brother were like two bossy foremen with one laborer to boss. As the job moved along, pieces of plaster began falling on my head. I began trying to dodge them. My uncle sarcastically said, "What's the matter? Afraid of a little plaster in your hair?" Then they began throwing debris haphazardly toward me after I refused to stand below the contact points of their chiseling. Both began to laugh and mock me for not being an obedient, empty-headed laborer willing to take their verbal abuse. "Don't you want to get dirty doing a *real* man's work?" they scornfully inquired.

My uncle and brother were two high school dropouts who took a sadistic pleasure in ridiculing me. They had not a clue about the intellectual pressure I was under trying to catch up in my four courses and saw no value whatsoever in education. My mother saw what was happening and gave me no flack when I told her that I would not be a part of their mockery anymore and returned to my academic work. With that episode, I lost any respect I had for my uncle, and my relationship with my brother would be permanently altered.

For the next two years our family would live there until my mother decided it was just too much work and expense to turn the house around and bring it back toward its impeccable condition in the late 1950s when my grandmother had been alive. At the time my mother owned her house, credit cards were still rare; everything you purchased had to be paid for with cash. Although my uncle unselfishly helped her with some of the major structural problems, the list of things needing to be repaired or replaced was just too extensive. And neither my brother nor I had yet learned how to do basic home maintenance and renovation.

* * *

Chapter Eleven

A New Spring Approaches

After purchasing my 1963 Triumph Spitfire in December 1966, I stored it in the garage my uncle Frank and grandfather had built on our College Street property in the late 1950s. On March 1, 1967, I officially put my sports car and motorcycle on the road. The weather would be breaking, the snow would be gone, and I would be able to have a couple of different means of transportation, which I thought would help increase the time I could spend with Marilyn. Being together, talking and communicating, and sharing intimate time would most certainly help us to get back on track, I believed.

But many nights I found myself driving home after spending time with Marilyn feeling hurt and frustrated at not being able to improve our relationship. I knew with complete certainty that I loved her with all my heart. I believed she felt the same way as me, but some demon, some cunning devil, was influencing her. Did she love me as much as I loved her? In my heart and soul, I was certain of this. But there was something else going on beyond my eighteen-year-old's level of comprehension and maturity.

Just one year earlier, we had been living together in the most romantic, loving environment imaginable, which we had created by ourselves. There were no extraordinary complications, and we had managed to live, know, and feel the simplest, purest love two people could express together. Every day was ours, and the outside world was not allowed to interfere. Our focus was on our relationship and the sanctuary we had jointly created. Again and again my mind would return to the simplicity and perfection of that golden time we had spent together.

There began to be blocks of time when we couldn't get together. Between her work schedule and my school schedule, something always seemed to interfere. On free nights, when I wasn't able to see Marilyn after my classes ended in early May, I would go to the Tudor Lounge next to Laughlin's Bar on Franklin Street. It had become a landmark and was the place to go to hear good music (in the background), have great conversations, and be near the epicenter of the growing love power/hippie/counterculture movements that were germinating across America. The cross-section of people was quite incredible. You met students, professors, professional people of all sorts, young people, old people, blacks, Hispanics, whites—everyone was there in one exceptional throng. Electricity was in the air.

Mercifully, in those days the music was clearly in the background, and every single spoken word was audible. It was not uncommon to engage in an extended discussion about politics, philosophy, or the growing movement against the war and have it last several hours. Once you were drawn into a conversation, you found yourself so focused on what was being said that your surroundings seemed to disappear. When the discussion concluded and you became aware of your surroundings again, you'd be amazed at the size of the crowd that seemed to have magically appeared and at how much time had passed. There was intellectual passion and fervor all around, and people genuinely wanted to talk about the topical issues affecting us. There was an urgent need to communicate what we were witnessing and what was happening to our world. The bar scene became a forum and gathering place for critical conversations about the political and social issues of contemporary America.

Many of us believed that we could not be passive, simply accepting the judgments and consequences of actions taken by the older generation. The world was out of joint, and we needed to talk about it, to try to fix it. We didn't want to be unquestioning lemmings or mindless automatons accepting whatever fate others tried to impose on us. The young people of our generation began an unnatural daily ritual of reading the obituary page for the names of friends and former classmates who might have been devoured by the war raging in Southeast Asia. Real concern and passion fired our intellect.

Into the Vibrant Social Scene

Come on baby, light my fire
Try to set the night on fire, yeah
From: "Light My Fire" by The Doors

In those days, there were no tape players for cars. I owned a seven inch speaker, reel-to-reel (battery or A/C operated) portable tape player. On my reels I had recorded whole albums of music by Bob Dylan, Joan Baez, Simon and Garfunkel, and a new group called the Doors. The sound quality was quite rich for a large one-speaker system. The unit fit nicely on the jump seat behind the two front bucket seats of my Triumph. My car became a kind of mobile jukebox sharing my intense music with anyone in earshot. My friend Butch (my former high school dropout partner) and I began to hang around together when Marilyn wasn't able to be with me. We started spending time with other friends at Tudor's about the time my first semester of college was ending.

Butch seemed to show up in my life when things were going wrong to provide much-needed distraction for my mind. In fact, it was Butch who first brought the Doors' first album to my attention. His cousin Sonny, who owned a handmade leather goods store on Elmwood Avenue called Sole Source, had turned him on to them. "Light My Fire" could be heard everywhere and was a monster hit almost immediately. Although it was essentially a fervid love song, it captured the intense passion for life that filled the air in the summer of 1967.

Butch introduced me to Lou R., a young philosophy doctoral candidate from the University of Buffalo who was the partner of Tom P., a high school English teacher who taught at my old high school. Lou would have an influence on my academic direction, and we often engaged in stimulating conversations spanning philosophy, contemporary issues, and life in general. These elucidating discussions usually took place in crowded bars or restaurants over the next several years. As the *in place* migrated from the Tudor to Blackstones, Brinks, Mulligan's, and then Mr. Good Bar, we would discuss academic philosophy and the impact of the antiwar movement. Lou's rational, clear-thinking approach to any subject matter was an inspiration to me.

By the end of my first semester, my relationship with Marilyn had become confused and out of focus, but the energy of new ideas from academia and the electricity of passionate discussions about contemporary life began to infuse my intellect with an enriched and enhanced vigor. I began to feel I was seeing life with what Dylan Thomas referred to as a *blinding sight*. I started to feel the compulsion to act upon what I was seeing. My intellect was like a lithium battery being charged to full power, and there would soon come a time when I'd begin discharging that stored energy, along with many other young people of my generation, at the contradictory forces in our society. This process of stimulation and assimilation of ideas was incredibly exciting.

Yet a vacuum was beginning to separate Marilyn and me. She had changed jobs again and was now working at another hospital, this time in North Buffalo. I began to perceive a distance and a slight aloofness in her that I had never seen before. After living with Ellen Jo for a few months, she again moved back to her parents' house. She had been coached by Ellen Jo and had her head filled—with what pearls of wisdom I couldn't say.

When we were both free from work, we would go out. Marilyn's work schedule dictated when we'd be together, and most often, it was on the weekend. Ellen Jo's influence was apparent, and I could feel a distance growing between us. While this intolerable alienation was growing between us, the outside world had grown both exhilarating and dangerous. The Vietnam War, like a vast sinkhole, kept opening wider and wider, swallowing more and more young men of my generation. We were continually being told that it was righteous and good, but the firsthand stories and casualties said otherwise. Literature questioning and opposing the war began to appear and to be discussed, especially among students and teachers on and off campus.

You're old enough to kill, but not for votin'
You don't believe in war, but what's that gun you're totin' ...
From: "Eve of Destruction" by Barry McGuire

The music of our generation grew passionate and pointed, and it took on the verve of a crusade, first by questioning the validity of the war and second by examining the value system of our whole American way of life, which was driven by a soulless capitalist dynamo bent only on fueling its continued growth and wealth. *War is good for the economy*, we were told. Humanity be damned! Nerve ends were struck, and steps were taken to suppress the message of our music.

Barry Maguire's "Eve of Destruction" was banned by most commercial radio stations. (Ironically, years later it would be played on the same stations as a *golden oldie*.) Some of the music, which questioned the motives and righteousness of our leaders and the profiteers hiding in the shadows, reached levels of near-critical perfection but never aired on popular AM radio stations. Bob Dylan's "Masters of War" and "With God on Our Side," although recorded before the Vietnam War escalated out of control, unmasked the key paradoxes in the slogans used to motivate well-intentioned, patriotic young men to kill one another. The platform for this new genre was *underground* FM radio stations, and it would take several years to have them expand across the country and to have enough listeners to influence our political system.

Publications like *Ramparts Magazine* presented articles that revealed sinister forces lurking behind popular myths about the unquestioned goodness of America. Che Guevara's murder, orchestrated by the CIA, exposed a world heretofore unknown to us. Questions, serious questions about who America was, began to surface. And the more questions we asked, the greater the efforts to suppress my generation. The pressure to silence the growing dissent increased across the antiwar movement and the civil rights effort. Arrests increased, and leaders of these movements were demonized in the biased popular media. Some were killed and some arrested, but all became targets of misinformed hatred.

> *You that never done nothin'*
> *But build to destroy*
> *You play with my world*
> *Like it's your little toy ...*
> From: "Masters of War" by Bob Dylan

On campuses across the country we'd hear the *other* stories not aired on the commercial radio and television stations or in the corporate newspapers. Without fail, the versions we heard came from actual participants in those events and told a very different story. We came away with a healthy skepticism of popular media. Our basic beliefs were under attack. Suddenly, we found ourselves feeling as though we were living in a Nietzschean universe where absurdity and pessimism prevailed and hope was nearly hopeless. The world seemed to be filled with lies and myths about who we were as a country and a civilization. In a few short years, our youthful optimism would morph from a sanguine lightness into a foreboding pessimism.

I think it's time we stop, hey, what's that sound
Everybody look what's going down ...
From: "For What It's Worth" by Stephen Stills

Political Pressure Grows/A Generation Seeks Escape

A sense of urgency fueled life in 1967, and that energy would flow like a swift river into 1968 and reach a crescendo by the end of 1969. From the creative forces in music to everyday life, the imprint was visible everywhere. As pressure about the war was exerted on my generation, you could see the need for escape begin to take its toll. Drinking increased, and a newer source of escape became popular: drugs. First it was marijuana (a.k.a. pot, weed, smoke, etc.) and then later a string of more potent drugs. Smoking pot allowed us to detach from the fatal thoughts about our lost brothers and friends and the prospect of our own peril. We could laugh easily, sometimes at pure nonsense. And laughing, no matter how ridiculous, was preferable to the alternative. For a few dollars, pot was purchased and joints rolled and smoked, creating a temporary oasis from the bleak world enveloping us.

Countless people moved on to LSD and mescaline—the psychedelic drugs. The people using what was referred to as *hallucinogenics* were popularly referred to as *heads*. These rebellious young people tended to have longer hair and wilder clothes, and they were less connected to the normal working world. In those days your appearance and lifestyle would preclude you from finding gainful, regular employment. Many of my friends and peers from that era became low-level drug dealers to finance their lifestyles. The idea of taking hallucinogenic drugs and *tripping* for a long period of time did not appeal to me, although I would briefly experiment with hallucinogenics a couple of years down the road.

Friends spoke about their visual observations and seeing a fantastic world while tripping. Perceptions were heightened, and self-awareness and self-consciousness could reach frightening depths. Some said you could release your worst insecurities to a point where you were unable to separate them from reality. It was like you were having a nightmare you couldn't awaken from. While tripping, one could see fantastic images and have epiphanies that revealed profound truths, or one could experience horrific visions augmented by deep insecurities. The latter often required intervention by friends or, in more serious cases, hospitalization.

Lots of my friends smoked weed, and some dropped acid or mescaline. The harsh reality of life (and death) grew more and more frightening, and discussions about our plight as draftable men grew increasingly frequent. Some of the fringe group began entering the world of hard, addictive drugs: codeine, cocaine, and heroin. Members of that group were easily distinguished by their constant activity to fill their habits. They were seen either in a drug-induced stupor or walking around nervously looking for a random opportunity to steal anything that could be pawned for cash to buy their next fix. On occasion, girlfriends of some of these hopelessly hooked junkies would be for sale for cash.

I felt sorry for the lost souls who'd been reduced to this zombielike single purpose in life. I couldn't imagine how good their drug high could be to lead them to live so low. It was said that their drug high was like no other high, but the low that followed was worse than hell itself. The thought of injecting a dirty needle full of liquid poison into a vein was worse than any situation one could face in life. At least, that was my take on it.

As spring approached the summer in 1967, an episode began to unfold that brought my life into close contact with the world of heroin addiction. I was able to see just how dehumanizing it could become and how someone I personally knew could be transformed from a young, vibrant, beautiful person into a hopeless soul living day to day, unable to break the cycle of heroin highs and hellish lows.

Marie V. was the younger sister of one of my friends, Joe V. She was quite attractive, with long, light brown hair, brown eyes, and a lean, shapely body. She was bright, and the sound of her laughter was sweet and drew you toward it. Her smile was a perfect physical parallel to the sound of her laughter. At some point, probably in the summer of 1966, she began to get involved with an acquaintance of mine, with whom I played high school football and graduated from Grover Cleveland High. Don N. was a popular guy who was a member of one of the other high school frats at our school. He was well liked and, I would say, an above-average student who wasn't quite committed to applying himself to his studies.

Once graduation from high school occurred, our class scattered in the wind: some off to faraway colleges, some to local colleges, some to join the effort to stop the domino spread of godless communism in the jungles of Southeast Asia. Don N. wasn't a part of any of these groups. Once Laughlin's and Tudor Bar (located side by side) became the nexus for socializing in the spring of 1967, Don began hanging out there, generally outside the bar on the sidewalk. Many people (myself included) would go outside the usually packed premises to get a whiff of smokeless fresh air and garner a bit of space. Don was often with Marie, Elroy D. (a tough kid we had also graduated with), and another guy who was short, dark, and muscular and whose name has long since faded into the recesses of my memory.

This group of outsiders was not part of the cadre inside the popular bar. They often huddled together like immigrants in a foreign country, by themselves for the most part, and if you approached them they'd only exchange niceties. They were on a different mission than most of the people inside the crowded bars. After a few months, the word circulating was that Don's group was not interested in alcohol, pot, or hallucinogenics but had become serious heroin users who had been seen with known addicts and dealers from the East Side. A stigma hung over his group like a poisonous fog. Once a popular, likable figure, Don was now *persona non grata*.

By the late summer, Don wasn't seen as often at the Franklin Street scene. Marie started showing up with another woman I had previously met that summer whose name was Edna G. She was an attractive, dark-haired, late-teen woman with smooth, tanned skin and could be fun to talk to—unless she was drunk. When Edna got drunk, she became very belligerent and verbally hostile if someone crossed her path. I had witnessed intelligent people who tried to dazzle her with their intellect get verbally ripped apart by her.

On one occasion, a few months before I had ever seen her with Marie, she needed a ride home when the bar was closing. I offered her a lift to her North Buffalo home. On the way, we engaged in a general conversation about our lives and some of the challenges facing us. I felt empathy for her. She was facing inner turmoil and issues I could only imagine. She was troubled, and I acted like a brother to her, which she seemed to genuinely appreciate. She knew I wasn't trying to play her for any dark motive.

Whenever I ran into Marie and Edna, sans Don and his street posse, we spoke about general things. I perceived some darkness around them and couldn't help myself from talking about the importance of gaining control of their lives and living a meaningful life. I felt very passionate about this simple philosophy, which, I suppose, was a form of religion without a god. I spoke with a heartfelt, positive passion and sincerity. I really liked both of them and felt an affinity with their hearts and sincere concern for their plight.

For a couple of months I would often show up at Tudor Bar and find them already there, ready to descend upon me to talk about their lives. I was flattered by their attention, so on one occasion when Marie asked me for my home telephone number (which was actually my mother's phone number on College Street), I gave it to her. I didn't think anything about it until she began calling me at odd hours, once at three a.m. On that occasion, one of my sisters answered the phone and came to my room to tell me that Marie was calling and wanted to speak with me. Exhausted, I said: "Just tell her I can't talk right now."

The next time I saw Marie at the bar, she told me that she had really needed to talk to me and that because she couldn't, she had shot up heroin. Of course, I felt a sharp pang of guilt, but I tried to explain to her that she must find a way to deal with those terrible urges by herself if I, or someone else, was not available. I don't know what effect this had on her, but it was the best I could offer. I had almost always dealt with my own situations basically by myself. I had no idea about the power of her addiction demons. My good-willed, innocent naiveté was no real answer for the complexities of a heroin addiction. That topic was a dark subject which was not openly discussed.

Several weeks later, I ran into Marie at Tudor's, and she told me she had some great news. Out of the blue, she was getting married to Frank E., whom she really *dug*. Furthermore, she told me that they would be leaving for Japan, where they'd be spending a couple of years while Frank completed a tour of duty in the US Air Force.

I looked deeply into her eyes and asked: "Marie, do you love him?" Again she reiterated, "Oh, I really *dig* him!" I pointed out how critically important it was for any marriage to have love at its core to succeed. She must love him for it to work. She let me emphasize my point about love and marriage. Then she told me she had to go but asked me to call her. She wrote her phone number on a matchbook cover and said emphatically: *"I must see you before I get married!"*

That comment reverberated in my mind for quite a time, and something inside me said: *She wants you to dissuade her from marrying Frank so she can be with you.* I was in over my head, and anyway, my first and sole priority was to be with Marilyn—she was the one I loved and needed and must be with. Needless to say, I never called Marie or saw her before her marriage to Frank and their subsequent departure to Japan.

Frank and Marie were married and left for Japan just as she had told me they would. The next time I saw her was in the summer of 1970 on the streets of Allentown, near Mulligan's Brick Bar, hanging out with known hardcore addicts. The light in her beautiful eyes was completely gone, and I could sense that she had lived through unspeakable things. Mutual friends, who knew her and were privy to the details, told me that after marrying Frank (the man she really *dug*) and going to Japan, Marie quickly got involved with a group of African American servicemen who were heroin addicts. Japan was a strategic center for the movement of pure heroin from the Far East to America. Her husband, initially distraught about her drug involvement, ended up an addict as well. On their return home, they parted forever. She took to the streets, and I believe Frank turned his life around and moved on.

The eyes of a person so often reveal much about them. Marie's eyes had lost their special glow. She looked hard, and any sense of joy and innocence was completely absent. She had become an antonym for joy. Her spirit had been pulverized, and what was left was reduced to a simple single purpose in life. Her world was shattered. As she spoke to me, I tried to recall the person I had known at the Friday night dance at Mount Major, the person whose laughter radiated positive energy. I tried to recall the person who had struggled to free herself of her demons at Tudor's. I could not see that person in the form standing before me. She was so mutilated by her living nightmare that it was as if an alien inhabited her physical form. The tortured person standing before me was beyond any of my well-intentioned but simple self-help words of wisdom. Her life had moved into a complex sphere where words of concern had no impact. Our paths did not cross again.

The last news of Marie came from a portable radio on a Sunday morning in the summer of 1976. I was painting the outside of a friend's house when the newscast came on. "Marie V., the mother of a one-year-old daughter, was brutally tortured and murdered by a known drug dealer who found out she had turned informant to avoid jail time." Her infant daughter was in the apartment when the ghastly murder took place. The final stage of hopeless addiction had taken place. Unlike others who had overdosed and died, Marie met one of the other grim fates awaiting addicts who tried to avoid prison by informing on their dealers. Her death was nonetheless tragic and sad. I will always remember her glowing smile and the sound of her wonderful laughter while I lament the horrible waste of a life that should've been beautiful, full, and complete. Rest in peace, lovely child.

A Magical Door Opens/A Roof Caves In

In mid-June, after a period of inconsistent contact, Marilyn called me to tell me that she had spoken with her closest friend, Olga. Olga told Marilyn that she thought we should be together. I replied to her friend's opinion by asking her: "What do you think, because it sounds like Olga is more certain about our relationship than you?"

Marilyn agreed with Olga's observation and said with conviction: "We should be together." My heart filled with joy, and the magic of our love recast its spell over me yet again. It was a chance, another opportunity to reconnect and make things right.

For the next several weeks, we were together not only on the weekend but during the week. She was living back at her family's residence, and everyone seemed happy to see us reunited. Marilyn had acquired some beautiful new clothes, which she began wearing when we went out. She was a gorgeous young woman who looked stunning no matter what outfit she wore. She had a perfect shape, long golden blonde hair, and piercing blue eyes that made you think you were gazing into heaven. The sound of her laughter was a philharmonic symphony that enriched and touched the farthest reaches of my soul.

At night, we would go out in my Triumph sports car. We spent intimate time together as best we could without the privacy of an apartment. My whole being was drawn to her in every possible way. But the days of totally compatible, inexhaustible discussions about everyday activities had passed. She was a working woman strongly grounded in the working world, and I was a working college student whose everyday interests had expanded sharply into the theoretical and philosophical arena. My intellectual appetite had been enormously increased by my brief college exposure, and my whole life would be forever linked to it.

One of the great influences I had in my very first semester of college was a young, charismatic philosophy professor named George H. He taught introduction to philosophy (a freshman course), and I was immediately impressed by his ability to logically dissect philosophical issues and to raise questions in the search for truth. George taught me that knowing the question was often more important than knowing the answer. He never pretended to know the answers and, furthermore, showed his students that some answers may be unknowable. He opened the possibility of doubt and skepticism. We came from a black and white world, and George showed us the universe of gray. His inspiration would motivate me to go on to take another eight philosophy courses during my undergraduate studies and, at one point, seriously consider philosophy as my major for graduate school.

On one occasion, George used the word *dichotomy* (a division into two contradictory parts). It was one of those smart, rich, meaningful words that not only expressed an intellectual thought but also existed beyond everyday working class discourse. It instantly entered my vocabulary like a fine Bordeaux wine through my palate. I mention this now because that word, *dichotomy*, became a flash point and would affect the entire course of my life.

One evening after our reconciliation, Marilyn and I found ourselves sitting alone on her living room couch talking about general stuff. We had been out that evening, and I was spending my last few minutes talking with her. During our discussion she raised a point about something that I can no longer even recall. My response to her comment included this new and intelligent word in the form of the exact question George had raised in our philosophy class. "What sort of dichotomy is that?" I innocently asked her.

Her response was swift, painful, and, perhaps, cruel: "You think you're so smart! Well, if I had gone to college I would've gotten better grades than you!"

Her unexpected words hurt me deeply and completely. She had voiced a sharp resentment of my effort to alter my life and way of thinking by going to college. No member of my large family, or any of my numerous friends and countless acquaintances ever said anything so hurtful to me. What did she expect me to do: not enrich my life, not develop my potential, not transform myself? I felt as if an icy dagger had pierced my heart. If Marilyn wasn't behind my effort to get an education (which in turn would enrich my vocabulary, expand my way of thinking, and change me for the better), well, I was on my own, alone.

I left her house on G. Street and drove home lost in thought in my Triumph. Along the way, I tried to sort out the real meaning of her painful attack. My gut said I had had enough of her recriminations and I needed to stay away from her—for now. What happened to the person I had fallen in love with whom I wanted to spend my whole life? Why did she lash out so bitterly at me? Was I trying to belittle her by applying a word from the education I was striving to achieve? The answer from within the deepest part of my being was an emphatic: *No! No! No!* I was trying to *share* with her some of the intellectual joy I was experiencing. I loved her more than life itself and would do anything for her, anything! But I just couldn't bear having the most important person in my life demeaning my effort to transform myself.

Why? I kept asking myself. I could not answer the question and needed time to recover from the pain of her accusatory and piercing words. As I lay in bed that troubled night, tossing and turning, I finally came to the decision I had to back off for a while—for how long I didn't know. Where was the person who not long ago had proclaimed her love for me and the importance of being together? I needed some time and space to recover from her piercing and hurtful words, which had temporarily stunned my spirit.

* * *

CHAPTER TWELVE

Nightlife and Laughter as an Oasis

Color in sky Prussian blue
Scarlet fleece changes hue
Crimson ball sinks from view

Wear your love like heaven
Wear your love like heaven
Wear your love like heaven

Lord, kiss me once more
Fill me with song
Allah, kiss me once more
That I may, that I may
Wear my love like heaven,
Wear my love like heaven ...

Wear Your Love like Heaven
Written by Donovan Leitch
Copyright 1967 Donovan (Music) Ltd.

The summer of 1967 came to be known as the Summer of Love because of the outpouring of music inspired by the hippie movement in California, which tried to embrace a world based upon loving one another and had flowers as its central symbol. Young people from all over the country, and even young people from overseas, began migrating to San Francisco to be near the root of this thesis. Our generation was looking for a response to the increasing horrors of Vietnam and to the brutality and havoc aroused by the reaction to the civil rights movement. Flowers and *flower power* became the antithesis to the violence and injustice.

The passion of our music reached new heights and permeated all the radio stations, including the rapidly growing FM band. All the bars played the music, and all the local bands did their renditions of it. We became aware that our time was unlike any other. We found ourselves drawn into its magical, hypnotic trance. A collective search had been initiated by the madness of the war in Vietnam and the civil strife being violently expressed in major cities across America. Pandora's box had been pried open by the questions about the validity of the Vietnam War and the ongoing attempt to deny African Americans and the other minorities their basic civil rights. How could America be a great country if it denied its own citizens basic human rights?

Around the time of my separation from Marilyn, my friend Butch called me to go to Tudor Bar and to hang out. It was a place to get into discussions about the pressing questions of our generation, to hear our generation's ever-expanding body of music, and to distract my mind from the pain of the conflict between Marilyn and me. It was a refuge I could not resist.

We often engaged in serious talk—but not always. And we didn't always stay at the bar all night either. One night, a new acquaintance of ours, named Mike G., made a perfectly absurd suggestion at two a.m. while at Tudor's. He thought it would be a *wild* adventure if we all snuck into the zoo in North Buffalo and went swimming with the seals. We couldn't believe how utterly ridiculous his suggestion was, and, with no hesitation, we piled into two cars, one of which was my Triumph Spitfire, and headed five miles north to the Parkside Avenue side of the Buffalo Zoo. We were six young men on a lark in the middle of a warm summer night.

The only things separating us from the zoo were a six-foot-high chain-link fence and the existence of a lone night watchman shrouded in the darkness. We devised a plan to divert his attention on the southern end of the Parkside entrance a hundred yards away while Mike and I scaled the fence on the north end near the new giraffe house construction. The first part of our commando mission went off smoothly without a hitch.

Both of us could see a trembling beam of light from the flashlight of the frightened watchman being pointed toward our four fellow conspirators, who seemed to be doing a masterful job of creating the necessary diversion. We felt like we were pulling off some mindboggling caper (a James Bond caper!) that seemed certain to succeed. After scaling the fence, shirtless, Mike and I were on our bare bellies stealthily crawling over grass toward a paved path that would lead us to the seal exhibit in the center of the zoo and our aquatic objective. Like all plans instantly spawned after a night of drinking and madcap fun, ours overlooked a couple critical points. The first, and most important, one was the reaction of a night watchman when confronted by a band of unknown people in the dead of a warm summer's night.

While we proudly rested on the scratchy grass contemplating our masterful plan and imminent success, we saw the flashing lights of a speeding police car pull up behind us on the other side of the fence we had just scaled a few minutes earlier, in perfect position to block our retreat. As we lay there, we could see our friends on the good side of the fence fleeing toward our cars, which were parked out of sight on a side street. They disappeared into the night; Mike and I were left flat on the ground moments before multiple flashlight beams would be fixed on us. I could feel the sting of mosquitoes on my bare back and knew we had no other choice than to surrender by calmly walking toward the source of the light cast on us.

A gold-badged captain and a patrolman escorted us to their black and white police cruiser, led us into the backseat, and began driving us back to the precinct station about a mile away. It was all quite civilized and polite. The captain, who was tall and sitting in the front passenger seat, turned around and asked us with genuine and compassionate curiosity: "What were you kids doing there in the middle of the night?"

I felt lighthearted and truthful, so I instantly replied: "Well, I may as well tell you the truth. We were going swimming with the seals."

He looked at the patrolman driving the squad car and uttered: *"Oh my God!"* while shaking his head in disbelief. Then he slowly turned his gaze out the front windshield, trying to fathom the motivation for such an act. Clearly, this was a brand new, original response. He couldn't have been more shocked if I had said we were dating two chimpanzees.

We arrived at the station house in a few minutes, and the captain, who was a very decent, kindly man, told us he'd have to call our parents. I gave him my mother's phone number first, and he called her to inform her of my part in this nocturnal prank. "Hello, Mrs. Ferri, this is Captain _____. I'm calling you to inform you that your son Joe was arrested for breaking into the Buffalo Zoo." My mother, who was absolutely notorious for being a little unconscious when awakened from a sound sleep, acknowledged that I was her son and said something to the effect that she would speak to me about this business when I got home. The captain had a puzzled look on his face when he hung up the phone, probably not certain why she had been so calm and so brief.

The captain then called Mike's father, whom I had never met. Mike's dad implored the captain to bring us to his house, about a mile away from the police station, so he could give us a real dose of necessary punishment in person. We were escorted back to the patrol car and, in no time it seemed, were at Mike's house on Amherst Street near Delaware Avenue. His father, who was a lawyer and sightless, opened the door and let the whole group into his living room. Mr. G., who was in his pajamas, bathrobe, and slippers, sat on one of the living room chairs as he listened to the captain describing our offense. Once our *crime* was revealed, Mr. G. began scolding us in a loud, stern voice for our stupidity and foolishness and pointed out the error of our way. He wondered out loud how he would punish us.

Then, in a seamless maneuver, he engaged the captain (who was in his fifties like Mr. G. himself) in a short, sporadic conversation mentioning this cop and that cop in between his tirade and outrage at us. Within a few skillful minutes, he had established that they had many mutual friends and that, by the way, this whole episode would be best handled by the parents of these clearly misguided youths. The captain acquiesced and was out the door with the patrolman in a flash, probably thankful that no police report needed to be written describing the misadventure of two young men attempting a deep night dip with a dozen seals. I'm certain the captain was convinced Mr. G. was going to physically trounce us.

As the door closed and our former captors drove off, I held my breath while I sat next to Mike on their couch, awaiting what was about to be unleashed upon us. I slowly lifted my embarrassed and timid gaze from the oriental area rug and looked at Mr. G. Instantly, his stern countenance was transformed, and he burst out laughing. He simply said: *"Be more careful in the future!"* through a liberating laugh.

I couldn't believe my ears. Mike and I left his father's house so he could drive me back to my West Side home. I told Mike, "You have the coolest father I've ever met!" I made up my mind that if I ever needed the services of a brilliant attorney, Mike's father would be on the top of my list. He was a perfect blend of thespian, counselor, and flimflam man.

The next day, after waking up in midmorning, I assured my mother that my late night gaffe was nothing to be concerned about and that the thought of swimming in the seal enclosure, with a slimy residue in the water and a cacophony of a dozen barking seals, was a sobering enough deterrent going forward. Mom believed my explanation, and the episode would be referred to and laughed about at family gatherings for years to come.

After leaving my mother's house on foot, I went looking for Butch, my other partner in crime, who had snapped into immediate action at the first sign of the police and made a hasty escape in my Triumph Spitfire. The Your Host Restaurant (often called "Your Host" or simply "The Host") in the West Side Plaza was a gathering place for many of the teens in our neighborhood. People would congregate there to talk about teen social issues. Sometimes they met members of the opposite sex, but mostly, people would just sit around and b.s. for laughs. I decided to begin my search for my missing friend and car there.

Sharing a Special Place of Inspiration

A couple of years earlier, in late April 1965, before I had met Marilyn, I found myself at The Host after midnight having coffee and engaging in the usual small talk with the handful of assorted night owls. One of the girls, Anita N., whom I didn't really know to talk to, happened to be among our chattering little group. When she found out I had a motorcycle, she asked me if I would take her for a ride. Anita was a year or two older than me, had dark glistening hair and a pretty face, and was in great physical shape. She was brighter than most of the other teenage women who hung out at The Host. I had never really spoken to her before that night, and I, too, had grown bored with the predictable direction of the conversation in the restaurant.

She hopped on the back of my Yamaha, and I started driving in the direction we were facing. "Where do you want to go?" I asked.

She replied, "Anywhere you'd like." The West Side, although my home turf, was not all that exciting to drive around. If someone who didn't appeal to me wanted a ride, I would simply drive through our neighborhood streets and loop back to our starting point. I had constant requests for rides, and it got so bad that I often left my motorcycle home rather than being an amusement ride for every person I said hello to.

But Anita was a little older and, it seemed to me, more interesting than the usual suspects at The Host. She was attractive and a bit mysterious, a combination that prompted me to take her to one of the special places I'd visit to be inspired. We drove to Porter Avenue and then westward down to the Niagara River, where the final evidence of winter remained. Because of the ice boom, which spans across the river from the United States to Canada and holds back the Lake Erie ice pack, the final floe of ice sat in the Black Rock Channel.

Once we approached the waterfront, the late April night air, which had been unseasonably warm, cooled drastically. Anita held me tightly for warmth as we drove along the western end of LaSalle Park looking at the melting ice pack. I stopped my motorcycle, put it up on its kickstand, and then walked with her to the short chain-link fence. We easily scaled it and sat down on the concrete wall eight feet above the Black Rock Channel. We sat close together with our bodies touching. While we gazed out at the odd shapes and sizes of the ice mosaic in the water below us, we spoke about general things. I found her attractive and enjoyed feeling her left leg and hip touching the corresponding right side of my body. We could hear the soothing, crackling sound of the slow melting ice as we gazed beyond the old break-wall, commissioned by Teddy Roosevelt, toward Canada.

Our conversation was a far second to just sitting quietly and solemnly while observing the natural process of ice dissolving and moving imperceptibly slowly. This was nature's wake for the passing of yet another winter, and we had reached a tacit appreciation of this expression of her power. We both were humbled by our physical juxtaposition to this amazing process. It's in times like that when your self-awareness is heightened and you can feel the hand of infinity touching your soul. Those are special moments you can never forget and go back to time after time in your mind.

We hugged and kissed a couple times as we continued to sit upright on the wall with our feet dangling over the edge, but by then our bodies were too chilled to consider more than that. I liked her; she was truly different than most of her peers and possessed an intellectual depth that drew me toward her. Once we started getting too cold, we exited our little perch, and I drove her home. I held the back of her head as I kissed her good night from the seat of my motorcycle. We didn't talk about getting together again or trying to see where either of us would be on the weekend. We simply agreed that it had been a fun drive and a good time. Like a dream, it ended.

I would not see her again for five years. By then, the world, our worlds, would be completely changed and our circumstances transformed beyond anything either of us could have imagined. After those two innocent encounters, we would vanish forever from one another's lives. But our night overlooking nature's awe-inspiring spectacle on the river would be forever etched in my memory. She, too, would be an intimate part of that beautiful and fantastic memory.

Locating an Outlaw Commando

It was a moderate walk to the Your Host restaurant from my mother's house, and when I got there in the midday warm sunlight, I spotted my British racing green sports car in the parking lot. When I walked into The Host, the guys and a few girls on the stools and in the booths near the entrance all started laughing. Butch obviously had told them about our little caper, which backfired. He escaped; I was busted.

When I inquired about his lightning-fast escape and the aftermath, he simply said, "It was every man for himself." He had booked with my car because he knew that I wouldn't be needing it the rest of the night. "Did it ever occur to you to call me in the morning at my mother's to make arrangement to return my car?" I asked angrily.

He calmly replied: "I knew you'd show up sooner or later at The Host." Unfortunately, he was right.

I retrieved my car keys, got in my car, and drove off. I soon noticed my gas gauge was now on *E*. Apparently Butch had made the rounds after escaping Buffalo's finest and, of course, had forgotten to put a drop of gasoline in the gas tank. The real reason he was at The Host probably had more to do with almost being out of gas than with his concern for returning my car. Although this little misadventure and its benign outcome pissed me off, he was doing me a great service that he would never be aware of.

This period of time was during my hiatus from Marilyn. I began to throw myself into the vivid night scene for relief from the painful confusion and uncertainty that my troubled relationship was causing. I found myself trying to run away, that is to say, to hide from any thought related to her. The part of me that loved Marilyn and wanted to be with her was the sensitive, artistic, passionate part of my persona. With her in my life, I wanted to explore everything deeply and exclusively with just the two of us. With my friends, the devilish part of my personality emerged. That other part of me seemed to thrive on making people laugh. When I made others laugh I too laughed, and it made me less sad inside. The superficial sound of laughter at that time concealed the keening deep within my heart.

Foreign Experience: A Seed Is Planted

During that July, I learned about an interesting and often-discussed folk festival that would be taking place in the Toronto area. The Mariposa Folk Festival was going to take place at Innis Lake, outside Toronto, over several days in August, with performances by Tom Rush, Buffy Sainte-Marie, and a host of other folk singers. Although Butch had no particular interest in the folk music scene, I convinced him it would be a great adventure and a possible way to meet new women. He agreed to go, and we put together some crude camping gear, scraped a few bucks together, and headed up north toward Toronto, a place neither of us had ever visited, around dinnertime on Friday night.

Butch had borrowed an old canvas tent, which, if properly erected, could've been large enough for the two of us, my Triumph sports car, and a small herd of dairy cows. He had never set it up, I had never set it up, and in the pitch-black darkness when we finally arrived at Innis

Lake, it was quickly converted into a makeshift mattress. There was no rain that night, but the morning dew coated us nicely.

On our way up to the festival on the old Queen Elizabeth Way (QEW), we got lost for a couple of hours around the outer suburbs of Toronto. Every time we got new instructions pointing us to Innis Lake, we'd invariably end up going the wrong way and needed to stop again for fresh directions. We got to a juncture where we seriously considered completely changing our plans and doing something else altogether. We had reached a point where neither of us would've been surprised if we had started seeing Rod Serling at the gas stations we stopped at to get our next set of new instructions.

So once again, we pulled off the highway we were on (the 401, 402, 403—who knew?) and into another gas station to get directions *one last time*. As luck would have it, two people who were getting gas and heading to the festival told us to follow them. God only knows what route we took. It was now night, pitch-black night, and all I remember is that we went from the Toronto area with millions of lights to a rural area where it was really, really dark. We drove down paved roads and then onto dirt roads, and at one point I bottomed out my Triumph, which left a rather nice puncture in my manifold. The car instantly began emitting an annoying and unpleasant sound that would have heads turning our way wherever we drove and necessitate a visit to Sammy's Auto Repair the next week.

We miraculously managed to stay behind our Canadian guides, who drove to the rustic wilderness where the outdoor festival was taking place. We actually got to see Tom Rush and Buffy Sainte-Marie that evening on a spectacular, cloudless night. I couldn't ever recall seeing a more star-filled sky in my life. The music was wonderful and filled the cooling country air as we absorbed all the elements around us: a large crowd of enthusiastic strangers, the scent of vegetation blended with invisible, sweet clouds of burning cannabis, and the infinite palate above us with trillions of glistening silvery-white points of light. Beauty like that frees one's inner spirit and quells one's troubled mind. The ambiance and serenity of those few hours made the tedious journey to get there worthwhile. My injured soul was soothed and given a much-needed respite from the storm that raged two and a half hours away.

After the performance there were parties all around the hillsides.

Everyone was camping, and bonfires could be seen blazing and flickering in all directions. We could hear the sound of diverse laughing voices combined with many guitars attempting to play a variety of favorite songs. Somehow, the odd combination of sounds wasn't all that unpleasant. Most of the other people seemed to be in a jovial and relaxed mood, but Butch and I were two real aliens in that living pastoral painting.

I possessed a decent, rudimentary knowledge of folk music, especially Buffy Sainte-Marie and the better known performers. I knew next to nothing about the amazing city of Toronto. Butch didn't know the difference between folk music and Charmin toilet paper, but he did share my lack of knowledge of Toronto. It was probably the first time we felt like true foreigners because of our naiveté and innocent ignorance. Neither of us was comfortable enough to really have a good time. So when morning arrived, we folded our Barnum & Bailey tent, tied it on top of the trunk of my car, and drove back toward Toronto in broad daylight. The new directions we received, along with visible road signs, helped us navigate into Toronto with little effort.

We did a quick drive through the city, marveling at the cleanliness, size, and architecture. Toronto was in transformation, becoming the financial capital of Canada. The infusion of money, the increasing population, and the dynamic of economic wealth and optimism was in full force. Our city, Buffalo, was beginning its slide in the other direction. We made our exit back down the QEW toward familiar surroundings. Although we had been in Canada for less than one full day, we had seen some amazing things and learned a little about ourselves. Anytime you travel to a new environment, you can learn much about yourself. Perhaps it's the introspection you're forced to do or the insecurities you feel when everything and everyone is new. It can be a growing experience. That's the way I felt about that first trip to Toronto.

All of our friends and acquaintances knew that we were going to this great event up past Toronto for the weekend, so, when we approached the Peace Bridge, I had a thought. We were not due back until late Sunday, and if we showed up early, we could end up being the butt of some serious ribbing and mockery. For example: "How was the two-hour concert that took four hours to drive to?" or "So you got lost, damaged your car, slept outside on top of your tent in the dew, and never met any girls—did you have a good time?"

Rather than risk the drilling we surely would receive for going so far for apparently so little, I suggested we drive past Buffalo and go straight to Point Breeze, where we could spend Saturday night. Three years earlier, Butch and I had hitchhiked there and had a great time. Friends we had made, who were in a frat-like club called the Jaguars, let us stay in their rented cottage from Monday through Friday during one rainy week in August 1964 while they attended summer school or worked back in Buffalo.

It was at that time that I met Hillary L., whose sorority had rented a cottage in front of the one where we were staying. Butch and I had the exclusive privilege to entertain and be with seven or eight sorority sisters. It was on that occasion I first made contact with an attractive young woman's intellect and felt the special invigoration of intellectual ideas and physical beauty mixed together into an addictive potion. It was just a taste of what would come one year later, but it made me aware of its existence and my desire for it.

So on the strength of that old memory, we drove to Point Breeze, where we planned to hang out at the beach, maybe meet some people, and spend our vacant Saturday night. In the three years that had passed, the former teenager haven had regressed into a *family friendly* summer resort. It now seemed tame and curiously bland compared to when we had our adventures there just a few years earlier. Or could it have been that because we were coming from an emerging world-class city like Toronto, our tastes had changed and Point Breeze now seemed strangely inadequate?

Our attempt to connect with people our own age wasn't successful, and we had no chance to get an invite to a cottage like in the good old days. That night we dragged the circus tent off its resting place tied on top of my Triumph trunk, flattened it on the sand and gravel beach, and plopped our tired bodies on it like two nesting sandpipers. It would have been much more comfortable to have gone home and slept in our own beds, but we would've lost face. Never underestimate the pride of two Italian American guys. When morning came, we finally headed home. Although we had been gone less than two days, it seemed much longer. For years neither of us mentioned to friends our little side trip to Point

Breeze. Decades later at parties, our friends would laugh hysterically at the details of our absurd misadventure.

My time socializing with Butch and my other friends continued into the beginning of August. The nightly activities brought laughs and temporary relief from the cauldron of passion and problems seething inside me. No one could have guessed I was in such pain and emotional turmoil within. I was the master of masking the troubles inside of me by making people laugh. It helped me to laugh, and when other people laughed, I found I could laugh too. It was a very important escape for me.

But in time, the laughter grew shallower and shallower until it no longer provided any relief from thoughts about Marilyn and my love for her, which was tearing apart my soul. The superfluous sound of laughter could no longer mask the feeling of my love for her that began consuming my every thought. The superficial veneer of distraction grew all but transparent.

With the passing of the days and weeks, and with the silence between Marilyn and me continuing, another unexpected development had started to unfold. I started to see women who began to remind me of her. I'd see the back of the head of a blonde woman and my heart would race, thinking it was *really* her. But it wasn't. More and more, I imagined someone was her when it wasn't. She'd appear in my dreams nightly too. Finally, it got to the point when I started thinking about her almost constantly, missing her more and more, needing her desperately. My excursion into the energized nightlife was now all but meaningless; I yearned to hear Marilyn's voice, to see her beautiful face, and to hold her in my arms.

* * *

CHAPTER THIRTEEN

To the Edge of Death Valley

On Sunday evening, August 13, 1967, the very night of our return home from our Mariposa Folk Festival/Point Breeze weekend and on the exact two-year anniversary of when I proposed marriage to Marilyn, I reached the inescapable conclusion that the break between us had gone on far too long. We needed to work out our differences and find a way to reestablish our relationship in its rightful place in our lives.

From my mother's house on College Street in Allentown, in my bedroom off the living room on the first floor, I pulled the telephone inside and closed my door for privacy. This had been the longest stretch of time—over four weeks—without any contact with her. I missed her so much I couldn't stand it any longer. My time away from her just proved to me how much I still loved and needed her. The world I shared with my friends was mortal; the world with Marilyn was transcendental. With my friends I felt like a kid; with Marilyn I was a man. With my friends I had good times, but with Marilyn I had real happiness.

I positioned myself in my compact bedroom with the door closed. The extension cord on the telephone allowed me the ability to pace back and forth, which I often did when I was either nervous or upset. I dialed her parents' telephone number, knowing they would be done with dinner. The phone rang two times, and, to my slight surprise, Marilyn answered. I asked her how she was doing, believing that she must be having a parallel experience to mine. She replied in a slow, high-pitched voice, "I'm okay." I couldn't detect in her any sign of pain or grief, or even a slight echo of what I was feeling inside.

I was a little confused. My heart was pounding rapidly, and I refused to engage in a meaningless conversation about trivial stuff; my heart couldn't take it. Without hesitation, I told her I missed her, needed her, and loved her. I asked her when could we get together to try to work through the confusion that had occurred the last time we were together. Her response, her next words, would cast a pall over me, would doom me to a darkness my developing mind never knew existed.

"Things have changed," she declared.

"What do you mean?" I said in naive confusion. She then spoke words that would reverberate throughout my whole life and fuel a despair inhabiting my being forever. "I'm sort of reengaged," she announced.

I stumbled against the wall of my bedroom and slid in slow motion to the floor. I sat motionless in stunned disbelief; my body went numb. I slowly uttered the word, *"Engaged?"* as if it were from another language I didn't understand.

She reaffirmed that it was true, and I responded like an uncomprehending child, "I love you with all my heart—don't you love me?"

Her answer was to again slowly and painfully say: "Things have changed."

As if her words had not been spoken and I had not been condemned to gloom, I asked if I could see her. I was trying to get past the horror of the last few moments, hoping to erase the grim reality that was beginning to grapple my heart and soul. No matter how bad life had been to either or both of us, the beauty and power of our love released a magical joy and happiness that the outside world could not penetrate. But instead of granting my urgent wish, she replied that it wasn't a good idea and, furthermore, said: "You probably shouldn't call me, either."

The rest of the conversation was a blur. In a state of utter shock I hung up the telephone, feeling as if I had just been informed by my doctor that I had a fatal, incurable disease. My mind and heart were completely thunderstruck. The rest of the night I remained in my bedroom with the lights off, unable to face anybody or say anything. I felt hollow and empty like a ghost and eventually slipped into a tormented sleep. Throughout the long night I kept waking with my face buried deep in my pillow to muffle the sound of my weeping. My burning tears left salty stains on my pillow. *This can't be. This just can't be happening!* I thought over and over and over again. The night dragged on endlessly and painfully.

The next day when I awoke from the long, tortuous night, the irony of the previous night's conversation haunted me. On the anniversary of our engagement, during the Summer of Love, I had been discarded and replaced by some mysterious stranger in just a few short weeks. *How could this be? How could this be?* I asked myself repeatedly. The confusion and hurt lingered unmercifully for weeks. What was my crime to warrant such a horrid punishment? Surely, I must have committed some vile transgression to justify this life sentence. I had no idea.

The fall semester was days away, and I had by then quit my job at the *Buffalo Evening News*, opting to be a dedicated, unemployed full-time student. I had instinctively realized that my formal education would need to take center stage, not only for a future career but to help me survive the peril I was facing in the enormous vacuum left by Marilyn's departure from my life. My darkest thoughts danced around the antique derringer given to me by a friend several months earlier. When I held it in my hand, I felt its cold, deadly metal, occasionally pressing it against my temple in a fatal rehearsal. I refused to rule out any possibility. I contemplated living, and I contemplated dying. This internal debate about life and death would relentlessly continue within me for several critical weeks, and no person would realize how fragile my existence had become and how much danger I was in. Yes, I was the master of disguise, creating illusions about the person the outside world thought it knew. But a vast void was pulling me toward it.

Epiphany in Purgatory

One day several weeks later, I awoke on a clear morning feeling something new inside of me. I had lived with the darkest thoughts and grief for weeks and weeks, but on this particular day I felt a ray of (could it be possible?) hope. Why I felt it, I can't say. But it was there inside of me. It generated warmth like a small flame, and my weary spirit began to stir as if thawing, as my hands and feet had in the sewing store on President's Day back in 1966. I now knew I wanted to live, to try to go on with my life. I removed my antique derringer from under my pillow and relegated it to being a novel knickknack.

The fall semester started, and I attended classes courageously. My studies became my primary purpose in life. My thirst for learning had grown tremendously since the end of my high school days, and I found myself hungering for more. I knew this was the only thing saving me from succumbing to the emptiness after Marilyn left my life. But my new purpose and hope couldn't alleviate all traces of her from my thoughts.

One day it came to me that maybe she didn't want to see me because doing so might rekindle her feelings for me. As the idea took hold of me, its plausibility went from probability to near certainty—at least in my mind. I thought that if she saw me face to face, looked into my eyes, saw my sincerity, and was reminded of the powerful love I had for her, she would come to her senses and come back to me. How could she not? Didn't we pledge our deepest love for life? We knew we were meant for one another, and we were true kindred spirits and soul mates.

> *Gimme a ticket for an a aeroplane,*
> *Ain't got time to take a fast train*
> *Lonely days are gone, I'm a goin' home,*
> *'Cause my baby just a-wrote me a letter ...*
> From: "The Letter" by The Box Tops

My simple plan was to meet her, unannounced, after she left work at five p.m. and candidly ask her to talk to me. She was working at Sisters Hospital on Saturdays, and I knew what time she left work to catch the first of the two buses to get home. Since I was going to see her, why not give her a special gift? I had purchased an antique mantel clock that chimed on the hour and half hour. Marilyn loved antiques, and this would certainly delight her. Further, I thought, *Why not dress up for this special occasion?*

I arrived at the designated spot along the route she walked to catch her bus a few minutes before she left work. While I stood there, I began to see myself from outside of myself: dressed in the blue suit I had worn for high school graduation, holding a cardboard box with an antique clock inside. Suddenly, this image of myself made me feel pathetic and ridiculous. I felt weak and stupid, and now I could feel the movement of time passing too quickly. She'd be coming out in moments and see me looking foolish and wretched. There was something terribly wrong about this. *It's a mistake, a huge mistake!* I thought. In a flash, I retreated to a spot that was out of sight.

Seconds later she appeared, crossed Main Street, and within a few minutes she disappeared on the downtown-bound #8 bus. I went to my car, feeling shocked and ashamed by my near miss but oh, so close to the incarnation of my love, my muse. Instead of driving home, I drove ahead of her bus to where she would catch her second bus. Again, I parked my car on a side street and then stood nearby out of view like a mope until I saw her reappear and disappear again. With a sense of complete failure, I drove back to my mother's house in Allentown feeling empty and absurd in the suit I had worn with Marilyn by my side to celebrate my high school graduation just fifteen months earlier. I felt like a defeated coward, but I knew that if she had rejected me in-person, face to face, the consequence would've rekindled my darkest thoughts and motivated a final act of self-annihilation. There was only one thing left to do once you reached the lowest depth.

My failed effort recast a grim spell over my spirit. There was no one I could turn to for advice or counsel. Only one person in the world knew how sensitive and passionate I really was, and that person was no longer in my life. I was completely alone and found myself fighting for a reason to go on living. Once more, the darkness of August 13 inhabited my frail soul. My nighttime dreams were filled with images of Marilyn and sometimes sadistically reunited us, only to be dashed by the conscious world awaiting me every empty morning. I was a tormented young man.

Afflicted Exile

I resumed attending classes. Learning had always been an exciting process for me, but now it took on a new and far more vital dimension: it was a distraction from the reality I was struggling to come to grips with. Day by day I attended classes, trying to allow the intellectual excitement of learning to meliorate my troubled mind. But again, after a period of progress in my healing process, I began to reflect on my failed attempt to meet Marilyn as she left work. I still believed that meeting her face to face would elicit the emotions she still had for me.

One day after class, I drove to where Marilyn caught her second bus in downtown Buffalo, parked my car on a side street, and stood in the entranceway of the old downtown YMCA, which rose seven stairs up from the sidewalk. Imposing fluted stone columns were on either side of the entrance, and I had taken a position just behind one of them. This allowed me to get an unobstructed glimpse of Marilyn without being seen by her. My pathetic plan worked exactly as I had foreseen: she appeared, stood for several minutes on the busy sidewalk, and then vanished into her second bus when it arrived. As I observed her, a thousand questions raced through my brain. I don't think I blinked once while I looked at her. My eyes hungrily and thirstily drank every second of observation. I loved her *"with a love that was more than love,"* and I desperately needed her in my life. But as I drove home alone, the feeling of loss seized me once again. What could I do? I didn't know; I just didn't know.

The next week, after living through another wave of sad resignation, I found myself in possession of yet another plan to make contact with Marilyn. After class, I once again drove to my secret vantage spot by the YMCA in downtown Buffalo to take up my sentry post just outside the gates of Eden, awaiting the arrival of the amazing woman who had captivated my heart and soul. But this day would not be the same; I would emerge from the shadows and granite seclusion into the light of day in plain view for Marilyn to see. This would be the defining moment, my last forlorn hope, my final prayer to my soul mate.

The time arrived, and she appeared across the busy street on the other side of the river of vehicles flowing between us. After only a moment, I summoned the courage to step out into the sunlight, walked down to the elevated third stair above the sidewalk, and gazed intensely at her. Immediately, I saw her looking in my direction, and our eyes met in a visual kiss. I felt frozen as if my physical body was suspended in space. She too was motionless, but there were no words or gestures. Her image blazed in my eyes. I tried to psychically will her to me, to plead with her to just give me a signal to end my expulsion from *our* Eden. I kept screaming inside my tortured head: *I love you, my darling—we can have a life of love together!* How long this trance and prayer lasted I cannot say, but I didn't want it to end.

The cruel sound of a bus, her second bus, blurted out as it momentarily blocked our view of one another. Once it passed by and pulled ahead to its stop, we again caught sight of each other still standing fixed in our footsteps. I perceived a grimace on her face as she turned her lowering head and slowly began walking up to and then into the bus. She entered the bus and took a seat on the western side, never turning back to look at me. As the bus slowly pulled away, spreading a black trail of suffocating smoke behind it, I could see the late-day sunlight gently cascading down her glorious golden hair as it moved farther and farther away from me. The bus engine groaned more and more loudly as it overcame its cumbersome inertia of rest. Then, too soon, the crying sound of its stressed-out motor dissolved into the chaotic chorus of the distant rush hour traffic.

I stood paralyzed in my steps until the bus, and Marilyn, were completely out of view. It was over. The greatest joy and love I had or would ever know had vanished into another world that I could not be a part of and was not welcomed in. I withdrew to my Triumph, got in, and drove home feeling as if I were leaving a funeral procession. The finality of the event, the certainty of this final rejection, pierced me as deeply as an assassin's bullet in my chest. There were no more tomorrows, no more anything. I was totally and utterly alone, and the feeling of loss would resonate throughout my entire life. A part of my soul died on the third stair of the old YMCA in the setting sunlight that dark, sorrowful day.

> *I awoke today and found the frost perched on the town*
> *It hovered in a frozen sky, then it gobbled summer down …*
>
> From: "Urge for Going" by Joni Mitchell

* * *

CHAPTER FOURTEEN

The Shadow Cast across a Lifetime

It would be years and years before our lives would cross again. In that long interlude, I would travel many roads, meet many interesting people, and be an active participant in my generation's movement to stop the madness of our time. I would hear and meet great poets, philosophers, activists, and authors and begin the process of seeing the outside world. But in that time, a conventional life would not be part of my world. My life would be about experiencing the world on many diverse levels while being guided by an uncompromising critical and analytical mind.

Throughout my extraordinary journey, the thought and memory of Marilyn lay just below the conscious surface of my mind. With little prompting, I would be reminded of the awesome power and depth of my love for her. Songs of our era would release intense streams of emotion into my consciousness. From Dylan to Donovan to Joan Baez, Simon and Garfunkel, and the Beatles, virtually all the music we enjoyed together would pierce me deeply when I'd hear it. New music by those same artists somehow attached itself to the body of the music we had shared and affected me as well.

A year after our breakup, as I slowly emerged from the shadow of my heartbreak, I was reminded of the enormous emotional power and life of our love. A song hit the airwaves in the summer of 1968 around the sad anniversary of my loss of Marilyn.

After all the loves of my life
You'll still be the one.
From: "MacArthur Park," lyrics by Jimmy Webb

The words struck my heart like a sizzling bolt of lightning, and tears fell from my eyes. I still loved Marilyn as deeply as ever, and the message of this song foretold what my world would be without her. My life was once again interrupted, and I began questioning the value and purpose of everything I was doing. As my introspection raced through my mind, I scoured every aspect of my existence looking for meaning and validity. Since the great cataclysm of 1967, I had submerged myself into the intellectual world in academia and in the real world. The power of those experiences gave me the ability to resist the fatal thoughts of the previous year when all hope had seemed gone.

"MacArthur Park" unleashed the powerful repressed emotion I still possessed for Marilyn and pitted it against my emerging intellectual inner self. Two gargantuan forces did battle within me; neither triumphed, but I felt the terrible pain of both sides' wounds. This, inevitably, would be the pattern of my life. The best I could do was to try to find another love, another person to share my world. And there would be many.

Living an Examined Life

In October 1971, I was involved with a young lady who left Buffalo to attend college in Oneonta, New York. Anna was a smart, attractive, and sensuous woman whom I started dating in June of that year. She had left for college, and fall was her first semester away from home. She came from a bourgeois family and had a wonderful laugh and a beautiful smile. We shared a special, bewitching chemistry. At that time, I was not enrolled in college and was running my own simple house-painting business. There were breaks in my college education, and this particular break would last until 1977, when I returned to the University of Buffalo until I finished my PhD in English.

Back in June 1969, in my second month of my fourth tour working at Bethlehem Steel, I was assigned to one of the mills where we made extra money as an incentive for tonnage. The more tonnage, the more incentive dollars. After being laid off back in March 1967, I returned for summer employment from May through August over the next three years. There were no other local jobs that paid as much as the steel mill, and I had grown accustomed to the routine and money, so it was a real no-brainer to work there.

Some people, especially the temporary summer *white hats,* as the college kids were called, did what they were told and had a real disconnect from their job at Bethlehem. In one of the mills we were referred to not by our names but rather by the number on our brass gate passes. In that particular mill, I was assigned the personal number of 299.

Every morning, after having our Job Safety Analysis (JSA) read to us, we would be given our work assignment for the shift. The JSA consisted of frighteningly obvious common-sense sort of advice. For example: When working by an open molten-hot ingot pit (temperature in excess of 2,000 degrees Fahrenheit), it's not wise to stand too close to the edge. It was a major test of composure, for those of us listening to the obvious information, not to burst into spontaneous laughter.

We knew that if we started laughing, we'd be punished with a crappy assignment for our shift. It was even a test for us to restrain ourselves when the subforeman read the daily JSA to us in one of the many work shanties scattered throughout the plant. Most of those subforemen were older and had spent many decades as loyal servants doing whatever the Bethlehem hierarchy asked of them. Their reward was to be promoted to subforeman status and to manage the groups of summer kids. Reading fluently in front of a crowded room of sometimes wiseass college kids was not a prerequisite.

During one of these well-intentioned meetings, as our subforeman *du jour* struggled through the text of that day's JSA, someone added an observation and complaint about the high summer temperature predicted for that day. Our elderly boss for the shift tried to find a positive thought and responded in a thick Polish American accent: "It may be hot: but it's bedder-den-rain."

The crowded little shanty exploded in laughter at the famous phrase: *bedder-den-rain.* It immediately became a response to all sorts of comments. "They made me sweep the mill for four hours," someone complained. Response: "Well, it's bedder-den-rain." "I bought an egg sandwich at the cafeteria, and it was awful!" "Oh yeah? It's still bedder-den-rain."

The response became the comment for everything for our band of merry white hats, and it was applied to life outside Bethlehem as well. Some of the guys got drunk the previous night and had a morning hangover. We reminded them that their situation might be painful, but ...

On another occasion, as our assignments were being announced, my number was called out. Our foreman, Stanley, called my number, 299. But before he gave me my assignment for the shift, I interrupted him. "Listen, Mr. P., let me make a point here: all my friends call me 2." The room erupted in laughter, but the foreman didn't understand my comment.

So, in June 1969, I found myself working a production job with incentive pay, a position considered to be a privilege. By that year, I was fully engaged in the antiwar effort and was an unflinching and staunch supporter of the civil rights movement. I had been in many protest marches and attended trials of railroaded war resisters and civil rights activists.

I found myself working alongside several outstanding African American steel workers on one of the giant machines that produced pieces of steel with particular forms that puzzled me. I was one of those people who needed to know and understand what I was helping to produce. On a hot June night, while working the second shift (three to eleven p.m.), I was assisting an experienced machine operator stamping out oddly shaped pieces of steel. For the life of me, I couldn't figure out what they were or what they were used for.

After mastering my role of sliding pieces of metal beneath the crushing jaws of this loud, powerful piece of equipment, I decided I needed to know what I was helping to produce. I asked the black journeyman machine operator: "What are these things?"

"They're treads," came the response.

"Treads?" I naively responded.

"Yeah, for tractors and tanks," he said matter-of-factly.

"Tractors and tanks?" I repeated.

"Yep, tractors and tanks," he reiterated. I suddenly found myself gripped with a terrifying feeling and was almost afraid to ask my next question.

I looked at him, hoping I had misheard what he had said, and spoke the horrible word, *"Tanks?"*

"Yes, tanks—you know, for the military," he calmly clarified.

His answer nearly crushed me. The reality of this conversation raced through me like a moral firestorm. I was stunned and shocked. I instantly felt like Lady Macbeth with blood on my hands. For the remainder of my shift I was silent, but inside my head one of the great moral debates of my life was taking place.

Had I not participated in countless debates, antiwar demonstrations, and actions for the better part of the last three years? Wasn't I an active part of civil disobedience to protest against institutions supporting the Vietnam War? That night, I found I had a tangible connection to something I completely disagreed with. Up to that point, I had no connection to any activity directly supporting the war effort.

I was mortified by my part in the production of war materials. I hardly spoke another word and counted the minutes until my shift was over. Once it arrived, I walked out the gate, never to return to the steel mill. I disappeared, never to be heard from again by Bethlehem Steel.

Without a job, I was in desperate need of money, so I launched a house-painting business. I knew how to paint, but I had never run a business. I managed to get a few painting jobs, but they paid too little to prevent me from losing my apartment and my car. Although I hit hard financial times, I did not look back. I took a moral stand and paid the price. I did the right thing and never regretted it.

As for my house-painting business, I'd learn the various aspects of the business over the next couple years and achieve modest success. But, more importantly, I became independent enough to dictate the rules of my own life.

An Unanticipated Miracle

One night in early October 1971, when I was home alone in the Barton Street apartment I shared with my youngest sister, Camille, I received a strange phone call out of the blue. The caller, whose voice I didn't recognize at first, identified herself as Olga _____ (formerly Olga T.),

Marilyn's closest friend from her high school days. After the briefest small talk, she launched right into the reason she was calling: "Marilyn's getting divorced, and she asked me to call you to see if you would want to see her." My head began spinning at the meaning of those unimagined, unexpected words. I was speechless. She bluntly asked: "Do you want to see her?"

I was stunned and confused. My last image of Marilyn was seared into my heart and mind—her glistening golden hair moving away from me on a bus into another dimension to which I was not privy. I had been all but crushed by her departure and, for a critical period afterward, had seriously contemplated exiting this life to relieve the excruciating emptiness I felt. The void she left in my life had never been filled, nor would it ever be.

At that moment, I was being asked a most shocking and improbable question whose answer could transport me back in time. Although I was involved with Anna, I couldn't respond any other way but, *"Yes!"*

Olga gave me Marilyn's telephone number, and I promised to call her the next day. The last conversation I had with Marilyn was on Sunday, August 13, 1967. The sound of her voice, and the meaning of those painful words back then, had caused me enormous grief and changed the direction of my life. Virtually every woman I dated after her was either consciously or unconsciously measured against her image and many qualities. All my relationships were relatively short-term and left me unsatisfied as I continued to search for her replacement. But the sad truth, I would discover, was that there would never be one.

Searching for Her Double

My desire to fill the emptiness created by Marilyn's departure from my life led me to date younger women who shared traits similar to her. Most often, I'd date women with long blonde hair who were about five feet five inches tall and weighed about 115 lbs. Although I dated many women with those physical characteristics, it wasn't until a friend, Jack S., commented, "You always date women who look the same," that I realized what I was doing—and why. I was looking for a duplicate of Marilyn.

One summer night, my subconscious search for a Marilyn clone took a bit of a bizarre turn. Although I was out in the social scene, I had an aura of sadness and melancholy about me. The touch of darkness that surrounded me appealed to many women. When I was with a group of people, my mind played for laughs. But when I found myself with one or two people, my burning intellectual and passionate side revealed itself. I made friends easily, and having a sports car and motorcycle gave me an air of excitement. At the Tudor Lounge, I had met two lovely eighteen-year-old women who were best friends from the far East Side of Buffalo and recently graduated Catholic high school classmates.

Both of them had matured into attractive, sensual young ladies. I often spent time with them talking about everything imaginable. On a couple of occasions, I gave both of them a ride home in my sports car. They were both sweet and lovely, and I enjoyed their company—and nothing more. They knew I generally could be found at Tudor's at night.

When I arrived one night at about eight p.m., which was relatively early, I saw Elaine, the dark-haired friend of Melanie, standing by herself. The place was almost empty as we started talking. It appeared like it was one of those weeknights when the bar wouldn't get very crowded and end up being rather boring, so I asked Elaine if she'd like to take a ride with me in my sports car. We started driving along the water past the smelly fog of the Bethlehem Steel Mill. In a short time, we were on Route 5 heading southwest along the Lake Erie shoreline. Almost as if my Triumph was on automatic pilot, we drove and talked until we reached Point Breeze.

I took the old blanket out of the trunk of my car, and then we walked along the coarse sand and pebble beach. In a couple minutes, we went around a point of the beach that opened into a little cove, the very cove where one of my greatest memories had taken place. I opened the blanket in the center of the concise, intimate space, and we sat down. Our conversation soon dried up, and we began to embrace and kiss as our bodies lay pressed together.

A brief time later, our initial contact had escalated into a passionate exchange and culminated in one great climax. As quickly as it had begun, it ended. Once our hormones achieved their objectives, one of the two prostate bodies lay quietly on the blanket in the dark. Elaine kept holding me tightly and kissing me repeatedly. I lay almost passively, becoming conscious of the sound of water a few feet from our bodies. I felt no need or desire to reciprocate the emotional gestures Elaine was expressing. It felt hollow, and I was ashamed that I had allowed myself to get to that point. I felt sorry for Elaine because I knew she wanted this encounter to be the genesis of a great love. It seemed awkward and empty to me.

Shortly afterward, I suggested that we leave the beach and head back to the city. During our drive back, we made small talk. My inner voice chastised me for my weakness and for my lack of discipline. I really liked Elaine; she was bright and attractive, and I enjoyed talking with her. But there was no way our friendship would develop into anything romantic. My inability to control my libido that night angered me.

Once we approached the city, I decided I'd drive Elaine back to her East Side home. There was no exchange of phone numbers or even a hint of a plan to meet again. She knew where she could find me at night, and that was that. I scrupulously avoided any suggestion of encouragement. After I dropped her off and drove back toward downtown, I kept thinking about the disappointment I had probably created in her life. She would think our short, romantic tryst on the beach was some sort of beginning, but she'd be left to wonder why it would never be repeated.

It was still relatively early, so instead of driving home I went back to Tudor's. When I walked into the bar, there were more people than when I had left. It was about one-third full, and it was still easy to scan the crowd for any of my friends or acquaintances. Along one side of the bar, I spotted the blonde hair of Melanie, Elaine's usual accomplice and best friend. She looked in my direction, and once our eyes met, we moved toward one another. We hugged and kissed in a way that only implies friendship. I bought our drinks, and we began chitchatting.

The friends Melanie came with remained in the original area where I first saw her, as if deliberately giving us space. After several minutes of our light conversation, the words "Do you want to take a ride?" escaped from my mouth. We left the bar, walked to my car, and then drove off. As if the first part of the night had never happened, I drove past Bethlehem Steel and the rust-colored fog along the lake, back to Point Breeze.

Again, I parked my car, went to my trunk, and pulled out my old blanket. I took her hand, and we walked along the pebble and coarse sand beach back to the little cove. I spread the blanket in the exact spot it had been a few hours earlier, and we took our place on it and began talking. Several minutes elapsed before I found myself kissing Melanie. We embraced and kissed, and nature took its course. But unlike with Elaine, I didn't feel like immediately escaping from the secluded spot. I found myself pulling her close to me after we had reached our physical crescendo. Even though it was dark, I could still see her blonde hair in the dim moonlight, and I ran my fingers through it. I felt a closeness to her that I didn't feel toward Elaine. In the end, though, the enhanced feeling I felt disappeared, and I knew it was time to take my leave from this once-sacred spot. Once more, I drove back toward the city and then to the far East Side of Buffalo, this time to Melanie's house. We kissed good night, and, once again, no promises or plans were made.

Going to Point Breeze, to the secluded cove where Marilyn and I had begun our great love, was clearly an attempt to recreate the magic of June 4, 1965. With Elaine, the visit ended with our physical climax. My attempt with the blonde-haired Melanie, who was physically more similar to Marilyn, lasted a little longer but ultimately had no chance for success. There was no great conversation about poetry, music, nature, or life and the illusion quickly evaporated. This was one of the crystal-clear times that revealed how my life had been indelibly affected by my relationship with Marilyn. I knew what I had done—and why.

If I had met Melanie first that evening, I probably wouldn't have brought Elaine to Point Breeze. Being with Elaine at the cove aroused my physical passions and desire to be with Marilyn, so I brought a Marilyn look-alike back to the cove. But, in the end, I was left with the painful awareness that I had participated in a sacrilege at a holy shrine. It would be decades before I'd return to that cove where my greatest love had begun.

* * *

CHAPTER FIFTEEN

Two Worlds Converge Again

Now, more than four long years and a tremendous amount of living later, I was again talking to the most important person in my life, who had disappeared into a mysterious world I would never know. I listened to the sound of her voice with a combination of excitement and trepidation. She would never know how close to death I had been after she left my life. She'd never know the full extent of my love for her or the awesome power it would exert on my whole life. In 1971, I didn't even know just how incredibly powerful it was, although I intuitively sensed its enormity. We spoke nervously for a short time, neither of us believing our ears or the circumstances that had brought this moment to life. She was in the process of a divorce, had a young son, and lived in an affluent suburb of Buffalo. We made plans to meet the next day.

After I hung up the telephone in near disbelief, several conflicting forces explosively raced about, colliding in my mind. The feeling of shock still gripped me. It was as if someone who had died had reappeared, alive and exactly as in life. Her voice had somehow retained the same zest for life and ability to envelop me in its magical cadence.

Since our separation, my life had been filled with much living and experimentation. I had traveled and met many interesting people, and I had seen and participated in a mind-boggling range of cultural events. The experiences I had in 1969 alone could be the subject of an entire book. Living a boring, predictable life was not to be my fate. Would Marilyn view my unconventional journey with fright? Would she join me in my continuing quest?

Then there was Anna, my current girlfriend, who was away at college in Oneonta, New York. I felt an obligation to her to continue our relationship, although I was uncertain about its long-term future. She had attracted me physically, but she was not on the same intellectual tier as Marilyn. Anna's family was affluent, and I don't think her relatives ever really considered me as more than a temporary distraction. Anna was being groomed to meet someone on her economic and social level. I was just an interesting diversion along the way to her conventional, preordained future. But the physical attraction I had for her mesmerized me, and I was not willing to instantly terminate it. It wouldn't be right to her or me.

I needed to see and be with Marilyn and then try to evaluate my next step. After all, what if I severed my relationship with Anna and my reunion with Marilyn ended in failure? This would create another plateau of suffering in my life. I decided, for the time being, that neither must know about the other's existence. I would walk a tightrope. All my living and traveling could not have prepared me for what was about to happen.

Paradise Revisited

The next day I drove to Marilyn's house after dinner to see her and get acquainted with the world she now inhabited. I drove into her driveway at, of course, the exact prearranged time. As on our first date, no sooner had I arrived at our meeting place when she appeared, this time emerging from her house with the attached garage, walking toward me. She looked as beautiful as ever, and a slow, cautious smile appeared on her sensual mouth. Once I got out of my old white Ford Comet, our eyes, now at the same level, peered deep inside one another. My body trembled with a mixture of joy, relief, and fear.

This was the person I had lived for, the person whose presence in my life ignited all my senses, the person who inspired my greatest ambitions and most beautiful dreams, and the person who'd remain the central love of my life. Her magnificent, infinite blue eyes glazed over with tears as we embraced for the first time in a million years. While I held her in my arms, my body shook with a joy like a just-released prisoner in sunlight and fresh air for the first time in a long, long time. As we disengaged, we held hands tightly, as we had when we left the beach on our first date. She led me into her house and the world where her three-year-old son was waiting.

After a little time of distracted conversation with her son nearby, Aneil was brought to his room for bedtime. If the energy of my thoughts could've been harnessed as I sat alone on the couch in the living room, a small city could've been powered by it. There was so much to talk about, so much to find out about the eclipse we had lived through without one another. With her son safely and securely in bed, and soon asleep, the moment of revelation was now at hand. The impenetrable fog, which had existed between us since the darkest day of my life back on August 13, 1967, was about to be lifted.

Marilyn approached me; again our eyes glossed over with a powerful emotion. We kissed once, and our arms pressed one another tenderly but firmly. After we released, both of us wiped away our tears; then Marilyn began to reveal the details of her life after I had last seen her on the disappearing bus in the setting sunlight in downtown Buffalo in 1967.

Marilyn's strained relationship with her parents, but mainly her ancient father, had created an immediate urgency to find and make a new life. She realized while working at the hospital (and no doubt with Ellen Jo's influence) that her life could be transformed, almost instantly, if she married one of the many available young bachelor doctors she worked around.

Dr. K. came along in the summer of 1967. He needed an American bride for immigration reasons. The consequence of this union was a crass marriage of convenience. Real love was never to have a role. A child, a boy, was born about a year later, followed by the harsh reality of a loveless marriage to a man whose native culture thought of women as pure chattel and inherently inferior to men. Worse yet, American women were even lower down the totem pole, a disgrace, as it were. Dr. K. was of *royal* blood and coldly and arrogantly reminded Marilyn that she was not of his exalted class. In fact, she'd be a disgrace to his family back in India, and she should not expect to ever meet them.

She told me she knew that she had made a mistake marrying him, but, because she had gotten pregnant, she tried to make the marriage work. Her new world, instead of widening and expanding into incredible new areas, shrank into a small island. It was restricted and filled with pain and regrets, save for her son. Although material wealth would be hers, real happiness was not possible. Just finding simple contentment, too, was almost impossible. Her son would be her life until a point was reached when the marriage had to end.

Then she spoke words that nearly brought me to my knees. She told me in a passionate voice, "Joe, I *never* stopped thinking about you; I *never* stopped loving you." Tears fell from my eyes and from hers. My mind flashed back in time to when I had planned to intercept her as she left work at Sisters Hospital to confront her with my physical presence and pledge of undying love. She *never* stopped loving me, she said. If I had come face to face with her, our lives might have been dramatically different. We didn't meet that day. Years passed, and our lives took radically different paths. Now the knowledge that her love for me was as great as mine was for her overwhelmed me. Our hot tears touched one another's faces as we embraced and kissed again and again.

All those years I lived in exile from her, I had felt the same love for her. How cruel was fate to keep two lovers separated by a mistaken marriage for so long? Amazingly, our lives never crossed in shopping malls, restaurants, public parks, or on the street. I attended the University of Buffalo less than two miles from where she lived at the time of the breakup of her marriage. She told me that she had lived in Allentown for the first year of her marriage and was in walking distance of my new apartment, yet we never ran into each other. And since our separation, I had been pictured in the *Buffalo Evening News* and on local television stations at many protest rallies. She had never seen any of those images.

The Journey with a Moral Compass and No Map

In the years since my expulsion from *our* Eden, I had lived an interesting existence. I had traveled around the country and attended great concerts in Buffalo, Toronto, Newport (Rhode Island), New York City, and California. I'd been an active and enthusiastic member in the antiwar movement, participating in countless political rallies in several cities. I had worked to raise money for Biafra, had tutored inner-city students, and had worked on the presidential campaign of Gene McCarthy. I spoke the words of protest, and I engaged in the action those words demanded. I had lived the outrage and fervor of our time. The status quo had no place in my life, and I put myself on the front line at numerous political rallies.

My formal education was intermittent due to the changes in my focus and financial circumstances. As my involvement in the antiwar movement grew, I drifted away from formal academics. After that initial break from my university education, I would return two more times, but I was forced to leave after brief stints because it was necessary to work to support myself. I had no financial backing whatsoever, so I had no choice but to resign. My mother had given me tremendous moral support, but the school wouldn't accept it as currency. In fact, I'd always have to rely on myself completely to survive. Later, when I made up my mind that I must put school first in my life, I would achieve a prestigious Presidential Fellowship and a teaching assistantship that funded my PhD studies.

While at the University of Buffalo, I'd attend numerous poetry readings featuring such poets as Allen Ginsberg, Robert Creeley, Robert Duncan, Lawrence Ferlinghetti, Denise Levertov, John Logan, Michael and Joanna McClure, and many, many others. I'd meet political icons of the counterculture such as Jerry Rubin, Abbie Hoffman, William Kunstler, Timothy Leary, and Angela Davis (who picked me up while I was hitchhiking in Southern California).

My undergraduate focus, which was sparked by George H. at Buffalo State and Lou R. from UB, revolved around philosophy with a sharply leftist emphasis. Within that discipline, my questioning nature was given full license to examine every aspect of my personal life and the world I lived in. A relentless skepticism manifested itself in all my thinking. Gilbert Verret, a French protégé of Jean-Paul Sartre and a guest professor of philosophy at the University of Buffalo, further influenced my thinking. The absurd world that had confounded me in Dostoevsky's *Notes from Underground* became intelligible to me. My generation was surrounded by absurdity. Existential philosophy appealed to many thinking and questioning people of my generation, and it took root in my mind like a seed in fertile soil.

Since Marilyn's and my time together, my curiosity about life and need to know myself had fueled repeated odysseys outside the world of my youth. My love of topical folk music, and the desire to hear it firsthand, motivated me to travel to the Newport Folk Festival, to the legendary Gerde's Folk City and Fillmore East in New York City, and to numerous other venues to see and hear the great articulators of the questions of the 1960s. My travel became an ongoing pilgrimage to hear messages from the mouths of their creators and to be among the ever-growing audiences looking for answers and direction in our insane world. The sense of community among the expanding population of alienated young people started to be felt everywhere. The preposterous idea of a real revolution against our oxymoronic country began to feel real and inevitable. People spoke about it matter-of-factly, as if it were an unfolding reality sweeping away the present, clearly corrupt capitalistic system. In our minds it was real.

In 1969, the first year of the Nixon administration, the Vietnam War raged on, the protests continued, and the great questions about all of it continued to be posed in music, in poetry, and in letters. My generation found itself at musical gatherings to hear the music that articulated our collective outrage and to be among allies who found themselves being harassed and persecuted for their questioning nature. Many were treated as traitors for innocently and earnestly demanding answers to the urgent and critical questions of our time.

Once I rediscovered Toronto, it became one of my favorite destinations. In the Yorkville area you could go to the Penny Farthing Coffee House, drink coffee, and have lively discussions about the Vietnam War or civil rights movement with other patrons. Often, we'd connect with expatriates who had left America and their personal worlds behind to stay in the sanctuary of Toronto because the Canadian government refused to extradite war resisters. I would bring extra American cigarettes and newspapers from Buffalo to give to these Vietnam protesters from America, who welcomed any piece of life they had left behind.

The Woodstock Music and Art Fair (a.k.a. Woodstock) would be the great convention of our time. It was the pinnacle of the flower power and antiwar movements. People rallied together into a self-willed, self-made impromptu community. One of the announcers proudly proclaimed: *"We are now the second-largest city in New York State!"* The number of people converging on Bethel, an idyllic, sleepy little town, initially to hear music, became the focus of the entire world. Every major newspaper and every news outlet across America and overseas reported this event, which would never again be equaled in scope and uniqueness. The weather turned foul with heavy bursts of thunderstorms. But rather than spoil the mood of the enormous gathering, it spawned an instantaneous expression of unity. Everywhere you looked, you saw people helping their new neighbors by sharing food and cover from the storms. What the world witnessed was a spontaneous enactment of the tenets of the flower power movement.

For a glorious but brief time in August 1969, our war-weary generation demonstrated its message of peace and love to the world. Woodstock was proof of the validity of our message of brotherhood. If we work together for the greater good of all, we can overcome any obstacle and achieve anything. The message the world received from this great celebration of the counterculture could not be denied. "Peace and love" was not just an empty platitude. Woodstock demonstrated to the world, and ourselves, what we could be—if we wanted.

The year and the decade would end in 135 days. The impetus of the antiwar movement and emotions of the flower power era had, unknown to us, the participants, reached a crescendo at Woodstock. Many of the students had graduated or would be graduating from their colleges, joining the work force, getting married, and, ultimately, being absorbed into the world they had resisted year after year while enjoying temporary freedom from the strict world of their childhoods. The turning point had been reached, and the majority would willingly and voluntarily follow the certainty of the same old predictable path of their predecessors. It was safe and it was sheltered, but it was surrender nonetheless. *Moloch* sounded its siren, and the majority would respond. An epoch had ended without great fanfare and soon would melt into a narcissistic stupor. Too many people would change from reading magazines like *Ramparts* to fluff like *Self Magazine*.

> *Gotta get down to it*
> *Soldiers are cutting us down ...*
> From: "Ohio" by Crosby, Stills, Nash, and Young

In June 1970, I returned back to my roots in Buffalo after a three-month stay in Southern California. A new decade had begun. The zeal and passion of my generation, which had created a loud and distinct voice heard around the world, tragically began to become a whisper. The energy of the younger generation had forced President Johnson out of office, but now it began to rapidly and mysteriously dissipate.

One night afterward, while I was at a popular bar in Allentown standing by myself waiting for friends to arrive, Crosby, Stills, Nash, and Young's song "Ohio" began to be loudly played. Their moving and piercing words filled the crowded space, but the bar patrons were collectively turned off to the words and message and simply danced to the sound of the music. As I scanned the crowd from my elevated perch near the front door, I looked intensely through the faces below me, looking for a reaction to the lyrics from one face in the room. When my search ended in vain, I walked out the door and back to my apartment on Richmond Avenue. I was depressed and saddened because of what I had just witnessed and, more importantly, what it meant for the future. The fiery, passionate protests of the 1960s had somehow given way to a new era of a critical apathy, self-absorbed in superficiality. I felt as if I had just left the bedside of a dying friend. This terrible recognition throttled my spirit.

The Impenetrable Fog Is Lifted

Now, four years and two months after the most devastating event of my life, as I sat on the couch in Marilyn's living room listening to the tragic details of her attempt to escape the troubled world in her father's house, I felt enormous empathy for her. Since our breakup, I had never said or thought a disparaging word about her. I had somehow sensed that what she did back in 1967 had to be. Her leaving me was not because she didn't love me. Her actions, whose motives were unknown to me back then, were necessary for her very survival.

I now realized that my lifestyle, which was still evolving and without financial stability, was not a viable option for her at that time. She needed an instant solution to free her from the economic uncertainty and the negative emotional grip exerted on her by her father. My financial situation was a big question mark in 1967, so she chose a material answer. But I possessed a vibrant, compatible intellectual and emotional wealth that was completely absent from her marriage. The gulf between our two lives at once disappeared.

Our words turned into kisses, and soon we withdrew to her bedroom, where our bodies pressed together as tightly and passionately as when we lived together in our first apartment on Normal Avenue. We found ourselves embracing and kissing for hours. We made love with *Love* at its core—an experience truly different from and wonderfully superior to purely physical love. We could feel our essences reconnecting physically, intellectually, and spiritually. In the years since our lives were separated, this feeling, this magnificent feeling, had been absent from my life, and I had forgotten its amazing power. There'd be others in my life who would excite me physically and emotionally, but none ever approached the unfathomable depth I shared with Marilyn.

Marilyn, her son, and I would spend time together over the next few weeks. We'd visit two places, my two favorite regional places, which represented two diverse worlds that encompassed qualities of urban sophistication and awesome natural beauty, respectively. We traveled to Toronto in her new Saab and enjoyed the funky energy of Yorkville before taking an island ferryboat ride to Toronto Island for a picnic in the warm, early autumn sunlight.

A short time afterward, we would drive to another place Marilyn had never visited. We went to Zoar Valley (forty miles south of Buffalo), which was in full, vivid autumn colors, to have an Indian summer picnic near the shore of the sparkling Cattaraugus Creek. Zoar Valley is one of nature's great sculptures carved deep into the earth. Although people had lived there and tried to harness and tame her, nature always prevailed. The wild, enchanting beauty of the place would take your breath away. And the spectacular images that the colorful autumn scenery left in your mind would rival and radiate the same sort of wonder and inspiration as great artworks by the masters in major art galleries.

When we sat on our blanket spread in a picturesque field, we could see a harmony of hues in every direction. The sky was an intense blue like Van Gogh had captured on one of his canvasses. While we admired nature's celebration of vibrant colors and the wide variety of vegetation all around us, several untethered horses wandered past us freely and leisurely, sauntering to an unknown destination. It occurred to me that I was in the midst of one of the beautiful dreams that had haunted me from time to time. But now I wasn't sleeping; I wouldn't have to awaken to a cruel emptiness. This was *real*: Marilyn was with me in the warm sunshine. Her smiling face and her breathtaking beauty complemented the perfect natural splendor of this rustic Eden. I had unknowingly brought the queen of this pastoral kingdom back to her domain.

Marilyn's beauty glowed in the fall sunlight, and the sound of her laughter recast its magical spell upon me. As I watched her interacting with her son, I could see the great bond of mother and child. When she turned her gaze back toward me and our eyes met, I could feel our love and its special power. My love for this extraordinary woman had never diminished, had never been supplanted by any other woman I had loved. It became clear to me why I had never found anyone else. I had loved other women, but I never could go beyond a point because my love for Marilyn remained intact, deep within me. I never tried to feign love, so all my other love relationships were doomed to falter, to fade away—for all my life.

A Personal Dichotomy
and a Mistaken Choice

After a couple of weeks of spending intimate time with Marilyn, I had to confront the dual life I was leading. Living a lie, creating a deception in my relationships with Anna and Marilyn, had to be handled. This was truly unknown territory for me, and I relied completely on logic and reason. I hoped that my sincerity and honesty explaining this complicated circumstance to both of them would help all of us until some resolution and answer could be found.

Anna and I exchanged letters or telephone conversations regularly while she was away at school. Every second or third weekend she would either come home or I'd drive to the Catskills to see her. Through all this contact with her, I had an uneasy feeling about our relationship. Her world, both at school and at home, was alien to me. Many (if not most) of her friends came from affluent backgrounds and had advantages I had never dreamed of having. I was completely self-sufficient and relied on no family largesse. My personal wealth was my native intelligence and great passion for life. Anna seemed to recognize my unique intellect and was attracted to it.

The time approached for Anna and me to be together again, so I decided to drive up to her school to see her. Before I left Buffalo, I wrote Marilyn a detailed letter explaining, as best I could, the relationship I had with Anna, which existed before our reunion. I told her that I felt the relationship with Anna showed signs of ending, but at the moment, I did not want to end it abruptly, fearing that I might cause Anna lasting trauma like I had experienced when Marilyn had left me back in 1967. It was never harder to write a letter. I wanted to be as honest, open, and straightforward as possible while trying to figure out all the conflicting feelings crashing in my head. In the end, I wrote as sincerely as I possibly could and hoped Marilyn would understand.

Anna was quite a different story. I drove my old car 274 miles to Oneonta, New York, on a Friday afternoon. The wonderful, warm, and sunny Indian summer weather had ended, and a cold autumn rain replaced it. On my drive toward the Catskill region where her school was located, I reflected on a dozen different approaches to the inevitable conversation we must have about this unusual and terribly complicated situation. I knew in my heart that this weekend was going to be emotionally draining and unforgettable for all three of us.

Anna and I had dinner and spent our Friday night as we had spent every first night back together. It was good to see her and be with her. When I was with her, I felt the special tranquility and security lovers feel. She appeared to me to be innocent and at home in my arms; I felt needed in a way I just couldn't instantly walk away from. But when we were apart, I always sensed that she was another person, not the one who told me she loved me.

We made love and slept wrapped in one another's arms that night. In my head, I had rehearsed the conversation we would have to share on Saturday. Somehow, I must tell her the truth, or as much of it as I could. My hope was she'd understand and appreciate the dilemma I was facing and would bear with me as I attempted to sort it all out. All I knew for certain was that I had to be as honest as I possibly could be with her so she'd know I wasn't trying to deceive or mislead her. I did love her, and she needed to know that.

The next morning, after a sound sleep and with renewed energy,

I eased into the serious conversation that was exploding in my head. Anna listened attentively when she saw the pensive look on my face. I knew the words I was about to speak would have a profound effect on our relationship, but I had no other honest choice. As I spoke the words, "Marilyn has contacted me," I could see the innocent look on her face change to one of shock and fear. I had mentioned Marilyn, and the heartbreak of that relationship, to Anna back when we started dating. Anytime I entered a meaningful and committed romantic relationship, I spoke about my painful experience with Marilyn as a kind of statement of something I never wanted to repeat again.

Instead of asking me questions about the circumstances surrounding that contact, Anna began to cry—and she cried nonstop for two hours. Instead of discussing, as best I could, the details of this complicated situation, I essentially tried to find words to allay Anna's pain. By the time she'd stopped crying, I had reassured her that she had nothing to worry about and that I still loved her. I had spoken words to quell her fears and put her mind at ease. My sense of guilt and desperation to ease Anna's pain made me speak words that were not completely accurate. I did love Anna, but I loved Marilyn *"with a love that was ..."* My plan and mental preparation for this crucial and important conversation with Anna had been diverted to a compromised place. We spent the remainder of the weekend without ever bringing up the complicated subject again.

When I returned home after the weekend on Monday, Marilyn called me. The consequence of my letter to her was unknown. Would she accuse me of being false and some sort of terrible scoundrel? To my surprise, Marilyn told me that she understood what I was doing and "would wait for as long as it would take." I was flabbergasted; she understood the complex situation I was in and was going to wait. The maturity and love this displayed was astonishing. Our telephone conversations would continue afterward.

I found myself stuck between Marilyn's love and maturity and Anna's love and seeming innocence. Anna had made me feel guilty about hurting and misleading her. I just couldn't discuss with her the *whole* impact of Marilyn's return on me. And I felt terribly guilty about seeing her cry. Because of this, I tried to choose a path that would make Anna happy: namely, not seeing Marilyn in person, although we spoke daily on the telephone. This path would placate Anna, but it terribly frustrated Marilyn.

I had felt a degree of discomfort when I was with Marilyn in her home in Amherst which I didn't understand for many years. When I was with her, in her house or in her new car, I felt ill at ease. The house she lived in was the house she had shared with her husband, the doctor. The new Saab she drove and the alimony she received (which was many times what I earned painting houses) was a connection to her ex-husband. Even her innocent son was a reminder of the doctor. I felt an awkwardness and uneasiness being in contact with any of it. My fierce sense of independence made me feel an irrational guilt about any connection to it. Although my opinion was strong, I was wrong in feeling any guilt connected to those things. And whatever Marilyn's divorce settlement was, it could never have been enough compensation for the years she gave up to that wretched chauvinist.

For a short time, this arrangement I had with the two women continued. I spoke with Anna on the telephone and wrote letters to her that essentially continued to address the grief I had witnessed when she was informed about the return of Marilyn. It was as if I were trying to do for Anna what I had wished Marilyn would have done for me in the dark days back in August 1967. Anna seemed to respond to my effort at reassuring her of my love, but as this was giving comfort to her, it was hurting Marilyn.

On one occasion, during one of my regular phone calls with Marilyn, she got frustrated and abruptly hung up the phone. Trying to balance the two romantic relationships, while I frantically searched for a single solution to this complex situation, proved too much for me to handle. I was hopelessly caught in a dual guilt, and it seemed I was damned no matter what path I took. Logic and reason abandoned me, and I saw no way out. I took a coward's path and used Marilyn's hanging up the phone on me as a pretext to not call her back. After that conversation, I allowed silence to persist. Eventually, she vanished from my life again. Although my life seemed much simpler after this action (or inaction, as it were), it was perhaps the worst decision of my life.

I'd continue to see Anna and to give her my love and loyalty while she lived away from Buffalo, first at school and then working for an airline, only occasionally returning home to Buffalo. We talked about going to the next level in our relationship, but that conversation stayed in Western New York. After graduating from college, she would live in Utah and then Southern California and go through many romantic relationships. I'd see her from time to time when she came back home for brief visits or for family holidays. We had no future; I was just her homeboy to amuse her and entertain her during her layovers on home turf.

As it turned out, Anna had never been faithful to me. Almost immediately upon going away to school, she was with other men. By the time I found this out, it was several critical months after my last conversation with Marilyn. Anna's original response to my attempt to be honest and open with her, with regard to Marilyn, had made me feel a guilt that affected the delicate relationship I had with Marilyn. Ultimately, Anna's duplicity sabotaged my reunion with my real soul mate. Had Anna been honest with me back in the fall when I had divulged this complicated situation to her, I would never have stopped seeing and being with Marilyn; I would never have allowed any circumstance to separate us. Instead, years would pass before our lives would touch once more.

* * *

CHAPTER SIXTEEN

—

Dwelling in the Valley
and the Infinite Void

By 1974, I was running my modestly successful house-painting business in such a way as to accommodate my creative life. The off-season was during the winter months, usually some of November, most of December, and all of January and February. By March, I was able to gradually start the next outdoor painting season. When I was off from work, I used the free time to read and to write. My greatest interest was in poetry, so I spent time experimenting with verse, some of which was published.

Another pastime that stimulated my intellect was visiting the Albright Knox Art Gallery. It regularly inspired me to buy books to read about the artists I came to admire and respect. There was something fascinating about learning about the biographies of great artists and then seeing their work a couple of feet in front of you. When I read about them, I learned about myself. I saw parallels in our lives; after all, they too were passionate people with life experiences not all that different than mine. I began to see connections between great painters and great writers and the universal imperative to record observations and visions of life. I felt the rumbling of the creative process within me. Learning about their lives and worlds made me hunger for more knowledge.

One day during 1974, while I was shopping on Elmwood Avenue in Buffalo, I accidentally came face to face with Marilyn. She looked as beautiful as ever, and she smiled when our eyes met. She quickly told me that she now lived in East Otto, a small hamlet located in Zoar Valley (the place I had introduced to her three years earlier). She jotted down her phone number and told me to call her. She was leaving on a two-week trip to visit her brother Jimmy, who was stationed in Upper Michigan. I told her I would definitely call her and slipped her phone number into my wallet.

Several weeks later, I pulled out the slip of paper with her phone number on it to call her. I was embarrassed and ashamed by the way our last time together in 1971 had ended, and I wanted to see her again. Although my life wasn't a great financial success, I felt proud of my uncomplicated, creative existence. By operating my own simple house-painting business, I was able to avoid the usual ethical compromises that are often inevitable when working for a company or corporation. I consciously resisted the lure of the almighty dollar as a first priority.

So many people I knew had been absorbed by pure materialism. It reminded me of the 1950s sci-fi movie *Invasion of the Body Snatchers*. People fell asleep, the extraterrestrial entity entered their bodies, and by the time they awoke they had become emotionless and soulless alien creatures. I was able to keep my passion and creativity intact. My prime inner directive was to continue my search for knowledge and deepen my self-awareness. Sacrifices were necessary to keep this inner flame burning, and I willingly made them.

Now I had been given a chance to make contact with the only person I had loved with all my heart, whom I respected and, yes, needed in my life. From the moment we met on Elmwood Avenue, I planned to call her and to begin our relationship anew with *no* distractions this time. When the moment arrived, I took a deep breath and then dialed the phone number she had given me. My thoughts raced wildly in my head, and I knew I'd make plans to see her as soon as possible. I needed to explain to her how I had been misled by Anna as I struggled to figure out how to handle the complicated situation three years earlier. If anyone could appreciate my good intentions and genuine honesty, it was Marilyn. Yes, we had lost time, but couldn't we now make a real, uncomplicated effort to merge our lives? There was no question in my mind: we just needed a chance, one opportunity—nothing more.

After I dialed her phone number, while many questions danced in my head, I held my breath awaiting the inevitable ring of her telephone and then the warm sound of her inviting voice saying hello. Instead, a canned message came on: "This phone number is no longer in service; no further information is available ..." A new emptiness gripped me.

There was no happy Hollywood ending, no fairy-tale finish. For the final time, Marilyn would disappear from my life. Did I dream I met her on Elmwood Avenue? Was this last encounter a fantastic mirage in the mind of a lonely soul mate in search of the only thing that really mattered in his life?

All that remained were images of her stunning beauty, memories of her extraordinary brightness, and the magical echo of her glorious laughter. My heart would become the secret gallery storing those mementos of "a love that was more than love" for the length and breadth of my lifetime. I would never see Marilyn again, but my love for her would always remain with me, deep within my heart. As if I had made a deal with the devil, my most cherished wish and dream to realize a love as great as that in Edgar Allen Poe's "Annabel Lee" had been granted. But I had not read the fine print: I *must* lose her. And I would live decades longer than Edgar Allen Poe with the special emptiness and pain of the loss of my Annabel Lee, Marilyn.

On our first date in the hidden cove at Point Breeze, we listened intently to the song that moved our souls, inspired our hearts, and was forever branded to our love. Like so many young, fearless romantics, we embraced the beautiful lyrics of love but suppressed the ultimate sad sentiment of our song. Now, nine years later in the void created by Marilyn's final departure from my life, those dark, foreboding words of our song became the epitaph for our relationship and would haunt me evermore.

Catch The Wind

> *When rain has hung the leaves with tears*
> *I want you near to kill my fears*
> *To help me to leave all my blues behind*
> *For standing in your heart is where I want to be*
> *And I long to be*
> ***Ah but I may as well try and catch the wind.***

Catch The Wind
Written by Donovan Leitch
Copyright 1965 Donovan (Music) Ltd.

THE END